Contents

Spanish
Grammar

Beginner, Intermediate, and Advanced Levels

Third Edition

Christopher Kendris, Ph.D.
B.S., M.S., Columbia University in the City of New York
M.A., Ph.D., Northwestern University in Evanston, Illinois
Former Assistant Professor
Department of French and Spanish
State University of New York at Albany

Theodore Kendris, Ph.D.
Adjunct Instructor
Luzerne County Community College
Pennsylvania

*For St. Sophia Greek Orthodox Church of Albany,
New York, our parish
and
To the eternal memory of our beloved
Yolanda Kendris
who is always by our side
With love*

All inquiries should be addressed to:
Barron's Educational Series, Inc.
250 Wireless Boulevard
Hauppauge, NY 11788
www.barronseduc.com

Library of Congress Control Number 2010942481
ISBN: 978-0-7641-4607-7

Printed in China
9 8 7 6 5 4 3 2 1

How to Use This Book

In the chapters that follow, a numerical decimal system has been used with the symbol § (Section) in front of it. This was done so that you may find quickly and easily the reference to a particular point in Spanish grammar when you use the index. For example, if you look up the entry "adjectives" in the index, you will find the reference given as §5. Sometimes additional § reference numbers are given when the entry you consulted is mentioned in other areas in the chapter §. The index also includes some key Spanish words, for example *ser* and *estar*, and § references to them are also given.

About the Authors

Christopher Kendris has worked as interpreter and translator for the U.S. State Department at the American Embassy in Paris.

Dr. Kendris earned his B.S. and M.S. degrees at Columbia University in the City of New York, where he held a New York State Scholarship, and his M.A. and Ph.D. degrees at North-western University in Evanston, Illinois. He also earned two diplomas with *Mention très Honorable* at the Université de Paris (en Sorbonne), Faculté des Lettres, Ecole Supérieure de Préparation et de Perfectionnement des Professeurs de Français à l'Etranger, and at the Institut de Phonétique, Paris. In 1986, he was one of ninety-five teachers in the U.S. who was awarded a Rockefeller Foundation Fellowship for Teachers of Foreign Languages in American High Schools. His fellowship provided for summer studies in Europe in creative ways to teach Spanish and French.

Dr. Kendris has taught French at the College of The University of Chicago as visiting summer lecturer and at Northwestern University, where he held a Teaching Assistantship and Tutorial Fellowship for four years. He has also taught at Colby College, Duke University, Rutgers — The State University of New Jersey, and the State University of New York at Albany. He was Chairman of the Foreign Languages Department at Farmingdale High School, Farmingdale, New York, where he was also a teacher of French and Spanish. He is the author of numerous school and college books, workbooks, and other language guides. Among his most popular works are *French Now! Level One, Spanish Now! Level Two, Master the Basics: Spanish, Pronounce It Perfectly in French* (with three audio CDs of listening comprehension including tests with answers), and many others, all published by Barron's Educational Series, Inc. He is listed in *Contemporary Authors, Directory of American Scholars*, and in the author volume of *Books in Print*.

Dr. Theodore Kendris earned his B.A. in modern languages at Union College in Schenectady, New York, where he received the Thomas J. Judson Memorial Award for modern language study. He went on to earn his M.A. in French language and literature at Northwestern University in Evanston, Illinois, where he was a teaching assistant and senior teaching fellow. He earned his Ph.D. in French literature at l'Université Laval in Quebec City, where he studied the Middle Ages and Renaissance. While at Université Laval, he taught French writing skills as *chargé de cours* in the French as a Second Language program, and in 1997 he was awarded a doctoral scholarship by the Fondation de l'Université Laval. Dr. Kendris has also taught in the Department of English and Foreign Languages at the University of St. Francis in Joliet, Illinois, as well as at the Hazleton campus of Penn State University.

Dr. Kendris is the author of *Inglés completo: Repaso integral de gramática inglesa para hispanohablantes*, published by Barron's in 2008. He is also the coauthor of several language guides, including *Pronounce It Perfectly in French, French Vocabulary, E-Z French, 501 Spanish Verbs, Seventh Edition,* and *501 French Verbs, Sixth Edition,* also published by Barron's.

Preface

This third edition is one of a series of handy grammar reference guides. It is designed for students, businesspeople, and others who want to "brush up" on their knowledge of Spanish grammar.

Definitions and explanations are concise and clear. Plenty of examples use and reuse a core of basic vocabulary.

This pocket-size book contains essential Spanish grammar that is normally in the curriculum of beginning, intermediate, and advanced language study. It is a reference grammar review book of all three levels. We hope you enjoy, in particular, our section on "what prepositions go with what verbs" found on book pages 67–76. The complete grammar review consists mainly of the Basics, the Parts of Speech, and Special Topics, all of which are outlined in detail in the table of contents.

Here and there we offer some tips to help you remember certain aspects of Spanish grammar and vocabulary. For example, if you cannot remember that the Spanish word for twenty (*veinte*) is spelled with *ei* or *ie*, remember it this way:

Mnemonic tips are very useful in learning and remembering. Students learn and remember in different ways. What works for you may not work for someone else. You must think of ways to help yourself remember. If you think of a way that is helpful, let it work for you. One student told Dr. C. Kendris that she finally figured out a way to remember the meaning of *buscar* / to look for. She said, "I'm looking for a *bus* or a *car*." How many can you make up? Try it. It's fun! Here are a few more mnemonic tips. Some students confuse **hoy** and **hay**. See these pictures in your mind:

Tip	H [O] Y		H A Y
	T [O] DAY		T [H] ERE IS
			T [H] ERE ARE

You could also say: "*There is* **hay** in the barn."

The pronunciation of *hay* is like the English word eye. You don't remember the Spanish word for eyes / *los ojos*?!

Watch this: And this:

Tip (O J O) S   **Tip** A [Y] ER
                                   [Y] ESTERDAY

If we have omitted anything you think is important, if you spot any misprints, or if you have any suggestions for the improvement of the next edition, please contact the publisher.

Special thanks go out to Dr. Hilda Garcerán de Vall, a professor of the Spanish language and friend and colleague of Dr. C. Kendris. Her distinguished late husband, Dr. Julio Garcerán, was also a teacher of Spanish. They wrote the book *Guía del idioma español*, published by Las Américas Publishing Company. We sincerely appreciate her helpful suggestions while reading the manuscript to make sure that the Spanish contained in this book is *correcto como debe ser*, correct as it ought to be.

Christopher Kendris
B.S., M.S., M.A., Ph.D.

Theodore Kendris
B.A., M.A., Ph.D.

The Basics
Beginner Level

§1.

A Guide to Pronouncing Spanish Sounds

English words given here contain sounds that only approximate Spanish sounds.

	Pronounced as in the	
	Spanish Word	**English Word**
PURE VOWEL SOUNDS		
a	*la*	father
e	*le*	let
i	*ti*	see
o	*yo*	order
u	*tu*	too
DIPHTHONGS (2 vowels together)		
ai	*baile*	eye
ay	*hay*	
au	*aula*	cow
ei	*reino*	they
ey	*ley*	
eu	*Europa*	wayward
ya	*enviar*	yard
	ya	

	Pronounced as in the	
	Spanish Word	**English Word**

DIPHTHONGS (2 vowels together)

ye	_tiene_ _yendo_ }	**ye**s
yo	_iodo_ _yodo_ }	**yo**re
yu	_viuda_ _yugo_ }	**you**
oy	_oigo_ _estoy_ }	t**oy**
wa	_cuando_	**wa**nt
we	_bueno_	**way**
wi	_suizo_	**wee**k
wo	_cuota_	**wo**ke

TRIPHTHONGS (3 vowels together)

yai	_enviáis_	**yi**pe
yau	_miau_	m**eow**
yei	_enviéis_	**yea**
wai	_guaina_ _Uruguay_	**wi**se
wau	_guau_	**wow**
wei	_continuéis_ } _buey_	**wai**t

The accent mark (´) over a vowel sound indicates that you must raise your voice on that vowel sound.

	Pronounced as in the	
	Spanish Word	**English Word**
CONSONANT SOUNDS		
b	_bien_	**b**oy
	_va_	
d	_dar_	**th**is
f	_falda_	**f**an
g	_gato_	
	goma	**g**ap
	gusto	
k	_casa_	
	culpa	
	que	**c**ap
	quito	
l	_la_	**l**ard
m	_me_	**m**ay
n	_no_	**n**o
ñ	_niño_	can**y**on
p	_papá_	**p**apa
r	_pero_	Ap**r**il
rr	_perro_	bu**rr**, g**r-r-r**
s	_sopa_	
	cero	
	cita	**s**oft
	zumo	
t	_tu_	si**t**
ch	_mucho_	**ch**ur**ch**

	Pronounced as in the	
	Spanish Word	**English Word**
	OTHER SOUNDS	

h	_justo_ _general_ _gigante_ }	**h**elp

The letter _h_ in a Spanish word is not pronounced.

y	_yo_ _llave_ }	**y**es

Tip	The Spanish word **hay** (there is, there are) sounds like the English words _eye_ and _ay_.

The pronunciation given above is that of most Latin American countries and of certain regions in Spain.

§2.

Capitalization, Punctuation Marks, and Division of Words into Syllables

CAPITALIZATION

Generally speaking, do not capitalize days of the week, months of the year, languages, nationalities, and religions.

> *domingo, lunes, martes,* etc.; *enero, febrero, marzo,* etc.; *español, francés, inglés,* etc.; *Roberto es español, María es española, Pierre es francés; Elena es católica.*

PUNCTUATION

Common punctuation marks in Spanish are as follows:

> *apóstrofo* / apostrophe '
> *comillas* / quotation marks " "
> *paréntesis* / parentheses ( )
> *principio de admiración* / beginning exclamation point ¡
> *fin de admiración* / final exclamation point !
> *principio de interrogación* / beginning question mark ¿
> *fin de interrogación* / final question mark ?
> *punto* / period .
> *coma* / comma ,
> *punto y coma* / semicolon ;
> *dos puntos* / colon :
> *puntos suspensivos* / ellipses . . .

DIVISION OF WORDS

It is good to know how to divide a word into syllables (not only in Spanish but also in English) because it helps you to pronounce the word correctly and to spell it correctly. The general rules to follow when dividing Spanish words into syllables are:

In General

- A syllable must contain a vowel.
- A syllable may contain only one vowel and no consonant: *e / so (eso)*.

Consonants

- If you are dealing with single separate consonants, each consonant remains with the vowel that follows it: *mu / cho (mucho), ca / ba / llo (caballo), pe / ro (pero), pe / rro (perro)*. Did you notice that the consonants *ch*, *ll*, and *rr* are considered as one consonant sound and are not separated?
- If you are dealing with two consonants that come together (other than *ch*, *ll*, or *rr* as stated above), the two consonants are separated; the first remains with the preceding syllable and the second remains with the following syllable when they are split: *her / ma / no (hermano), at / las (atlas), ter / cer (tercer)*.
  But if the second of the two consonants that come together is *l* or *r*, do not separate them: *ha / blo (hablo), a / pren / do (aprendo), li / bro (libro)*.
- If you are dealing with three consonants that come together, the first two remain with the preceding vowel and the third consonant remains with the vowel that follows it: *ins / ti / tu / to (instituto)*.
  But if the third of the three consonants is *l* or *r*, do not separate that third consonant from the second; it remains with the second consonant: *com / pren / der (comprender), sas / tre (sastre), sal / dré (saldré)*.

Vowels

- Two vowels that are together are generally separated if they are strong vowels. The strong vowels are: *a, e, o*: *a / e / ro / pla / no (aeroplano)*, *o / a / sis (oasis)*, *re / a / li / dad (realidad)*.

  But if you are dealing with a weak vowel (*i, u*), it ordinarily remains in the same syllable with its neighboring vowel, especially if that other vowel is a strong vowel: *trein / ta (treinta)*, *ru / bio (rubio)*, *hue / vo (huevo)*.

- If a vowel contains a written accent mark, it becomes strong enough to remain in its own syllable: *Ma / rí / a (María)*, *re / ú / ne (reúne)*, *dí / a (día)*.

Other

- The letter *y* is considered a consonant when a vowel follows it. Keep it with the vowel that follows it: *a / yer (ayer)*, *a / yu / dar (ayudar)*.

Syllable Emphasis and Rules of Accentuation

(a) When a Spanish word ends in a vowel, the letter *n*, or the letter *s*, emphasize the second-to-last syllable of the word.
   Examples:

mu / CHA / cho	*re / SU / men*	*mu / CHA / chas*
(boy)	(summary)	(girls)

(b) When a Spanish word ends in a letter other than a vowel, *n*, or *s*, emphasize that last syllable.
   Examples:

com / pren / DER	*re / a / li / DAD*	*es / pa / ÑOL*
(to understand)	(reality)	(Spanish)

(c) Sometimes, a written accent (′) is placed over the vowel
that must be stressed, indicating an exception to the rule.
The accent mark tells the reader which vowel to stress.
Examples:

LA / piz (lápiz)	*DE / bil (débil)*
(pencil)	(weak)
LA / pi / ces (lápices)	*DE / bi / les (débiles)*
(pencils)	(weak)

Tip

> Most words in Spanish, including verb forms, end
> in a vowel, *n*, or *s*. Therefore, apply the first rule by
> keeping in mind the following tip:
>
> *El muCHAcho y las muCHAchas CANtan en
> espaÑOL.* (The boy and the girls are singing in
> Spanish.)

Note, finally, that *el corazón* (heart) requires an accent mark on
the vowel *o* because the pronunciation does not follow the
simple rule stated above. Spanish-speaking people pronounce
the word as *co / ra / ZON* with an accent mark on *ZÓN* to
show this exception. There are hundreds of Spanish words
that require an accent mark because their pronunciation does
not follow the general rule.

The Spanish Alphabet and the New System of Alphabetizing

The Association of Spanish Language Academies met in
Madrid in 1994 and voted to eliminate **CH** and **LL** as separate
letters of the Spanish alphabet.

Words beginning with **CH** are now listed alphabetically
under the letter **C**. Words beginning with **LL** are now listed
alphabetically under the letter **L**. The two separate letters his-
torically had separate headings in dictionaries and alphabetized word lists. Spanish words that contain the letter **ñ** are

now alphabetized accordingly with words that do not contain the tilde over the **n**. For example, the Spanish system of alphabetizing used to place the word **andar** before **añadir** because the ñ would fall in after all words containing **n**. According to the new system, **añadir** is placed before **andar** because alphabetizing is now done letter by letter. The same applies to words containing **rr**.

The move was taken to simplify dictionaries, to make Spanish more compatible with English, and to aid translation and computer standardization. Some of this information can be found on the web site of the Real Academia Española (*http://www.rae.es*).

The Parts of Speech

Nouns: Beginner Level

DEFINITION

A noun is a word that refers to a person, a place, a thing, or a quality.

Nouns are either masculine or feminine and normally require an article: *el*, *la*, *los*, *las*. See §4. about articles.

The gender of nouns that do not refer to persons or animals, where the gender is apparent, must be learned.

Gender	Noun Endings	Examples
masculine	-o	*el libro*
feminine	-a	*la casa*
	-ción	*la lección*
	-sión	*la ilusión*
	-dad	*la ciudad*
	-tad	*la dificultad*
	-tud	*la solicitud*
	-umbre	*la costumbre*
masculine or feminine, referring to a specific person	-nte	*el estudiante* *la estudiante*
some masculine some feminine	-e	*el aire, el coche* *la gente, la leche*

11

§3.1 IRREGULAR GENDER OF NOUNS

Ending	Gender	Examples
-o	feminine	*la mano* / hand *la radio* / radio *la foto* / photo
-a	masculine	*el día* / day *el drama* / drama *el clima* / climate
-ista	masculine or feminine, referring to a specific person	*el dentista* } dentist *la dentista* *el novelista* } novelist *la novelista*

§3.2 PLURAL OF NOUNS

Noun Ending	Plural	Examples
vowel	add *s*	*el chico* / los chicos
consonant	add *es*	*la flor* / las flores
z	change *z* to *c* and add *es*	*la luz* / las luces

§3.2–1 Other Exceptions

Sometimes a masculine plural noun refers to both male and female persons:

los padres / the parents, the mother and father

Generally, a noun that ends in *ión* drops the accent mark in the plural:

la lección / las lecciones; *la ilusión* / las ilusiones

Generally, a noun that ends in *és* drops the accent mark in the plural:

el francés / the Frenchman; *los franceses* / the Frenchmen

Sometimes the accent mark is kept in the plural in order to keep the stress where it is in the singular: *el país* / *los países*

Some nouns have a plural ending but are regarded as singular because they are compound nouns:

el paraguas / the umbrella; *los paraguas* / the umbrellas

Generally speaking, a noun that ends in *s* in the singular with no stress on that final syllable remains the same in the plural: *el lunes* / *los lunes*

Generally speaking, a noun that ends in *s* in the singular with the stress on that syllable requires the addition of *es* to form the plural: *el mes* / *los meses*

Some nouns that contain no accent mark in the singular require an accent mark in the plural:

el joven / the young man; *los jóvenes* / the young men

§3.3   SPECIAL CASES

§3.3–1   Nouns Used as Adjectives

It is common in English to use a noun as an adjective: a history class. When this is done in Spanish, the preposition *de* is usually placed in front of the noun that is used as an adjective and both are placed after the noun that is being described:

una clase de historia / a history class (a class of history)
una corbata de seda / a silk tie (a tie of silk)
un reloj de oro / a gold watch (a watch of gold)

Also note that the preposition *para* (for) is used in order to indicate that something is intended for something:

una taza para café / a coffee cup (a cup for coffee)

However, if the cup is filled with coffee, we say in Spanish:

una taza de café / a cup of coffee

§3.3–2   Nouns in the Diminutive

Nouns ending in *ito* or *illo*

Generally speaking, the ending *ito* or *illo* can be added to a noun to form the diminutive form of a noun. This makes the noun take on the meaning of little or small in size:

> *un vaso* / a glass (drinking); *un vasito* / *a little drinking glass*
> *una casa* / a house; *una casita* / *a little house*
> *un cigarro* / a cigar; *un cigarrillo* / *a cigarette*

To form the diminutive in Spanish, ordinarily drop the final vowel of the noun and add *ito (ita)* or *illo (illa)*: *una casa* / *una casita.* If the final letter of the noun is a consonant, merely add *ito* or *illo:*

> *papel* / paper; *papelito* OR *papelillo* / small bit of paper

At other times, these diminutive endings give a favorable quality to the noun, even a term of endearment:

> *una chica* / a girl: *una chiquita* / *a cute little girl*

Here, note that before dropping the final vowel *a* to add *ita*, you must change *c* to *q* in order to preserve the hard sound of *k* in *chica*:

> *un perro* / a dog; *un perrito* / *a darling little dog*
> *una abuela* / a grandmother; *abuelita* / "dear old granny"

Tip	In English, we do something similar to this:
	drop / droplet; doll / dolly OR dollie; pig / piggy OR piggie OR piglet; pipe / pipette; book / booklet; John / Johnny; Ann / Annie.

§3.3–3   Nouns That Change Meaning According to Gender

Some nouns have one meaning when masculine and another meaning when feminine. **Examples:**

el capital / capital (money)	*la capital* / capital (city)
el cura / priest	*la cura* / cure, care

el guardia / guard (person)
  el guardia de tráfico /
  traffic officer
el guía / guide, adviser
  (person)

la guardia / guard, watch
  estar de guardia /
  to be on guard, on watch
la guía / handlebar of bicycle
  la guía turística / tourist
    guidebook
  la guía de teléfono /
    telephone book

el orden / order, regularity
  llamar al orden /
  to call to order
el pendiente / earring
el pez / fish (alive in water)

la orden / command, order
  a la orden de /
  to the order of
la pendiente / slope
la pez / pitch (tar)

§3.3–4 *Campo, país, patria, nación*

The first three nouns (*el campo, el país, la patria*) all mean country. However, note the following:

- *Campo* means country in the sense of countryside:

    en el campo / in the country; *Vamos a pasar el fin de semana en el campo.* / We are going to spend the weekend in the country.

- *País* means country in the meaning of nation:

    ¿En qué país nació Ud.? / In what country were you born?

- *Patria* means country in the sense of native land:

    El soldado defendió a su patria. / The soldier defended his country.

- *Nación* means country in the sense of nation:

    Las Naciones Unidas / the United Nations

§3.3–5 *Hora, tiempo,* and *vez*

These three nouns all mean time; however, note the differences:

- *La hora* refers to the time (the hour) of the day:

    ¿A qué hora vamos al baile? / At what time are we going to the
       dance? *Vamos al baile a las nueve.* / We are going to the dance at
       nine o'clock.
    ¿Qué hora es? / What time is it? *Es la una.* / It is one o'clock.
    Son las dos. / It is two o'clock.

- *El tiempo* refers to a vague or indefinite duration of time:

    No puedo ir contigo porque no tengo tiempo. / I cannot go with you
       because I don't have time.

    Tiempo is also used to express the weather:

    ¿Qué tiempo hace hoy? / What's the weather like today?
    Hace buen tiempo. / The weather is fine.

- *La vez* means time in the sense of occasions or different
   times:

    the first time / *la primera vez;* this time / *esta vez; many times /
       muchas veces*

§4.

Articles: Beginner and Intermediate Levels

§4.1 DEFINITE ARTICLE

There are four forms of the definite article (the) in Spanish.

	Singular	Plural
Masculine	*el*	*los*
Feminine	*la*	*las*

They are:
Examples:
el libro (the book) / *los libros* (the books)
la pluma (the pen) / *las plumas* (the pens)

A definite article agrees in gender and number with the noun it modifies.

Noun	Article
m. singular	*el*
m. plural	*los*
f. singular	*la*
f. plural	*las*

If a feminine singular noun begins with stressed *a* or *ha*, use *el*, not *la*. For example, *hambre* (hunger) is a feminine noun but in the singular it is stated as *el hambre*. NOTE: *Tengo mucha hambre.* And NOTE:

> **Tip**
>
> *el agua* / the water; BUT *las aguas* / the waters
> *el hacha* / the axe; BUT *las hachas* / the axes

However, if the definite article is in front of an adjective that precedes the noun, this is not observed:

> *la alta montaña* / the high (tall) mountain
> *la árida llanura* / the arid (dry) prairie

Contraction of the definite article *el*:

When the preposition *a* or *de* is in front of the definite article *el*, it contracts as follows:

> **Tip**
>
> *a* + *el* changes to *al*
> *de* + *el* changes to *del*

Examples:

Voy al parque. / I am going to the park.
Vengo del parque. / I am coming from the park.

But if the definite article *el* is part of a denomination, part of a person's name, or the title of a work, there is no contraction:
Los cuadros de El Greco / El Greco's paintings.

§4.1–1 Uses

The definite article is used:

- In front of each noun even if there is more than one noun stated, as in a series, which is not always done in English:

    Tengo el libro, el cuaderno y la pluma. / I have the book, notebook, and pen.

- With a noun when you make a general statement:

    Me gusta el café. / I like coffee.

- With a noun of weight or measure:

    un dólar la libra; un peso la libra / one dollar a pound (per pound)

- In front of a noun indicating a profession, rank, title followed by the name of the person:

    El profesor Gómez es inteligente. / Professor Gómez is intelligent.

> **Tip**
>
> But in direct address (when talking directly to the person and you mention the rank, profession, etc.), do not use the definite article:
>
> *Buenas noches, señor Gómez.* / Good evening, Mr. Gómez.

- With the name of a language, it is optional to use the definite article: *Estudio español.* The trend in some Spanish-speaking countries is not to use the definite article when the name of the language is the object of a verb.

- With the name of a subject matter:

    Estudio la historia. / I study history.

- With the days of the week, when in English we use *on*:

    Voy al cine el sábado. / I am going to the movies on Saturday.

- With parts of the body or articles of clothing, especially if the possessor is clearly stated:

    Me pongo el sombrero. / I put on my hat.

- With common expressions, for example:

    a la escuela / to school; *en la iglesia* / in church
    la semana pasada / last week

- With the seasons of the year:

    en la primavera / in spring; *en el verano* / in summer;
    en el otoño / in autumn; *en el invierno* / in winter

- To show possession with the preposition *de* + a common noun:

    el libro del alumno / the pupil's book
    los libros de los alumnos / the pupils' books
    la muñeca de la chiquita / the little girl's doll

> **Tip**
>
> Note that when a proper noun is used, the definite article is not needed with *de* to show possession:
>
> *el libro de Juan* / John's book

- With names of some cities, countries, and continents: *la Argentina, el Brasil, el Canadá, los Estados Unidos, la Habana, la América del Norte, la América Central, la América del Sur*

- With a proper noun modified by an adjective:

  el pequeño José / little Joseph

- With a noun in apposition with a pronoun:

  Nosotros los norteamericanos / We North Americans

- With an infinitive used as a noun, especially when it begins a sentence:

  El estudiar es bueno. / Studying is good.

> **Tip**
>
> There are some exceptions: *Ver es creer* / Seeing is believing, and other proverbs. But you do not normally use the definite article with an infinitive if it does not begin a sentence:
>
> *Es bueno estudiar.* / It is good to study.

- When telling time:

  Es la una. / It is one o'clock; *Son las dos.* / It is two o'clock.

§4.1–2 Omission of the Definite Article

The definite article is not used:

- In direct address with the rank, profession, or title of the person to whom you are talking or writing:

  Buenos días, señora Molina. / Good morning, Mrs. Molina.

- After the verb *hablar* when the name of a language is right after a form of *hablar*:

    Hablo español. / I speak Spanish.

- After the prepositions *en* and *de* with the name of a language or a subject matter:

    Estoy escribiendo en inglés. / I am writing in English.
    La señora Johnson es profesora de inglés. / Mrs. Johnson is a teacher of English.

- With a proper noun to show possession when using *de*:

    los libros de Marta / Martha's books

- With an infinitive if the infinitive does not begin the sentence:

    Es bueno trabajar. / It is good to work.
    Me gusta viajar. / I like to travel.

- With a noun in apposition with a noun:

    Madrid, capital de España, es una ciudad interesante. / Madrid, capital of Spain, is an interesting city.

- With a numeral that denotes the order of succession of a monarch:

    Carlos V (Quinto) / Charles the Fifth

- With names of some countries and continents:

    España / Spain; *Francia* / France; *México* / Mexico;
    Europa / Europe

§4.2 INDEFINITE ARTICLE

In Spanish, there are four forms of the indefinite article. They are:

	Singular	Plural
Masculine	*un*	*unos*
Feminine	*una*	*unas*

The Spanish indefinite article is translated into English as a, an, some, or a few.

Examples:

un libro (a book); *unos libros* (some books, a few books)

una naranja (an orange); *unas naranjas* (some oranges, a few oranges)

An indefinite article agrees in gender and number with the noun it modifies.

Noun	Article
m. singular	*un*
m. plural	*unos*
f. singular	*una*
f. plural	*unas*

The plural of the indefinite article indicates an indefinite number:

unas treinta personas / some thirty persons

§4.2–1 Uses

The indefinite article is used:

- When you want to say a or an. It is also used as a numeral to mean one:

  un libro / a book or one book

  If you want to make it clear that you mean one, you may use *solamente* (only) in front of *un* or *una*:

  Tengo solamente un libro. / I have (only) one book.

- With a modified noun of nationality, profession, rank, or religion:

  El doctor Gómez es un médico excelente. / Dr. Gómez is an excellent doctor.

- In front of each noun in a series, which we do not always do in English:

    Tengo un libro, un cuaderno y una pluma. / I have a book, notebook, and pen.

- In the plural when an indefinite number is indicated:

    Tengo unos dólares. / I have some (a few) dollars.

§4.2–2 Omission of the Indefinite Article

The indefinite article is not used:

- With *cien* and *mil:*

    cien libros / a (one) hundred books
    mil dólares / a (one) thousand dollars

- With *cierto, cierta,* and *tal:*

    cierto lugar / a certain place; *cierta persona* / a certain person
    tal hombre / such a man; *tal caso* / such a case

- With *otro, otra:*

    otro libro / another book; *otra pluma* / another pen

- With an unmodified noun of nationality, profession, rank, or religion:

    Mi hijo es dentista. / My son is a dentist.
    Soy mexicano. / I am Mexican.

- When you use *Qué* in an exclamation:

    ¡Qué hombre! / What a man!

- With some negations, particularly with the verb *tener*, or in an interrogative statement before an unmodified noun object:

    ¿No tienes libro? / Don't you have a book?
    ¿Tiene Ud. libro? / Do you have a book?

- With a noun in apposition:

    Martí, gran político y más grande poeta . . . / Martí, a great politician and the greatest poet . . .

§4.3 THE NEUTER ARTICLE *LO*

Lo has idiomatic uses, generally speaking.
   It is used:

- With a masculine singular form of an adjective used as a noun:

    lo bueno / the good; *lo malo* / the bad
    lo interesante / what(ever) is interesting

- With a past participle:

    lo dicho y lo escrito / what has been said and what has been written

- With an adjective or adverb + *que,* meaning how:

    Veo lo fácil que es. / I see how easy it is.

§5.

Adjectives: Beginner, Intermediate, and Advanced Levels

DEFINITION

An adjective is a word that describes a noun or pronoun in some way.

§5.1 AGREEMENT

An adjective agrees in gender and number with the noun or pronoun it describes. Gender means masculine, feminine, or neuter. Number means singular or plural.

An adjective that ends in *o* in the masculine singular changes *o* to *a* to form the feminine: *rojo / roja, pequeño / pequeña.*

When an adjective that expresses a person's nationality ends in a consonant, it requires the addition of *a* to form the feminine singular:

> *Juan es español. / María es española.*

An adjective that ends in *e* generally does not change to form the feminine: *un muchacho inteligente / una muchacha inteligente.*

An adjective that ends in a consonant generally does not change to form the feminine: *una pregunta difícil / un libro difícil* — except for an adjective of nationality, as stated above, and adjectives that end in *-án, -ón, -ín, -or* (*trabajador / trabajadora*, industrious).

25

§5.2 POSITION

Normally, a descriptive adjective is placed after the noun it describes: *una casa amarilla*.

Two descriptive adjectives, *bueno* and *malo*, are sometimes placed in front of the noun. When placed in front of a masculine singular noun, the *o* drops: *un buen amigo; un mal alumno*.

A limiting adjective is generally placed in front of the noun: *algunos estudiantes* / some students; *mucho dinero* / a lot of money.

In an interrogative sentence, the predicate adjective precedes the subject when it is a noun: *¿Es bonita María?* / Is Mary pretty?

Some common adjectives have a different meaning depending on whether they are in front of a noun or after it.

Examples:

un nuevo sombrero / a new (different, another) hat   *un sombrero nuevo* / a new (brand new) hat
un gran hombre / a great man   *un hombre grande* / a large, big man
una gran mujer / a great woman   *una mujer grande* / a large, big woman
la pobre niña / the poor girl (unfortunate, unlucky)   *la niña pobre* / the poor girl (poor, not rich)
varias personas / several persons   *personas varias* / various (sundry, diverse) persons

§5.3 PLURAL OF ADJECTIVES

Like nouns, to form the plural of an adjective, add *s* if the adjective ends in a vowel: *blanco / blancos; blanca / blancas*.

If an adjective ends in a consonant, add *es* to form the plural: *español / españoles; difícil / difíciles*.

Tip	Note that the accent on *difícil* remains in the plural in order to keep the stress on the same syllable: *difíciles*.

Some adjectives drop the accent mark in the plural because it is not needed to indicate the stress. The stress falls naturally on the same vowel in the plural: *cortés / corteses; alemán / alemanes*.

Some adjectives add the accent mark in the plural because the stress needs to be kept on the vowel that was stressed in the singular where no accent mark was needed. In the singular, the stress falls naturally on that vowel: *joven / jóvenes*.

An adjective that ends in *z* changes *z* to *c* and adds *es* to form the plural: *feliz / felices*.

Tip	For a complete set of Rules of Accentuation, review §1. and §2. on pages 7–8.

If an adjective describes or modifies two or more nouns that are all masculine, naturally the masculine plural is used: *Roberto y Felipe están cansados*.

If an adjective describes or modifies two or more nouns that are all feminine, naturally the feminine plural is used: *Elena y Marta están cansadas*.

If an adjective describes or modifies two or more nouns of different genders, the masculine plural is used: *María, Elena, Marta y Roberto están cansados*.

§5.4 TYPES

§5.4–1 Descriptive Adjectives

A descriptive adjective is a word that describes a noun or pronoun: *casa blanca, chicas bonitas, chicos altos; Ella es bonita.*

Two or more descriptive adjectives of equal importance are placed after the noun. If there are two, they are joined by *y* (or *e*). If there are more than two, the last two are connected by *y* (or *e*):

> *un hombre alto y guapo* / a tall, handsome man
> *una mujer alta, hermosa e inteligente* / a tall, beautiful, and intelligent woman

§5.4–2 Limiting Adjectives

A limiting adjective limits the number of the noun: *una casa, un libro, algunos muchachos, muchas veces.*

§5.4–3 Demonstrative Adjectives

A demonstrative adjective is used to point out someone or something. Like other adjectives, a demonstrative adjective agrees in gender and number with the noun it modifies. The demonstrative adjectives are:

English Meaning	Masculine	Feminine
this (here)	*este libro*	*esta pluma*
these (here)	*estos libros*	*estas plumas*
that (there)	*ese libro*	*esa pluma*
those (there)	*esos libros*	*esas plumas*
that (farther away or out of sight)	*aquel libro*	*aquella pluma*
those (farther away or out of sight)	*aquellos libros*	*aquellas plumas*

If there is more than one noun, a demonstrative adjective is ordinarily used in front of each noun:

> *este hombre y esta mujer* / this man and (this) woman

The demonstrative adjectives are used to form the demonstrative pronouns. See §6.2 farther on.

> **Tip**
>
> To distinguish between *este libro* (this book) and *ese libro* (that book), remember that the *t* in *este libro* (this book near me) falls off on its way to *ese libro* (that book near you).

§5.4–4 Possessive Adjectives

A possessive adjective is a word that shows possession. It agrees in gender and number with the noun, not with the possessor. A short form of a possessive adjective is placed in front of the noun. If there is more than one noun stated, a possessive adjective is needed in front of each noun:

mi madre y mi padre / my mother and (my) father

There are two forms for the possessive adjectives: the short form and the long form. The short form is placed in front of the noun. The short forms are:

English Meaning	Before a Singular Noun	Before a Plural Noun
my	*mi amigo, mi amiga*	*mis amigos, mis amigas*
your (sing.)	*tu amigo, tu amiga*	*tus amigos, tus amigas*
your (sing.), his, hers, its	*su amigo, su amiga*	*sus amigos, sus amigas*
our	*nuestro amigo nuestra amiga*	*nuestros amigos nuestras amigas*
your (pl.)	*vuestro amigo vuestra amiga*	*vuestros amigos vuestras amigas*
your (pl.), their	*su amigo, su amiga*	*sus amigos, sus amigas*

In order to clarify the meanings of *su* or *sus*, when there might be ambiguity, do the following: Replace *su* or *sus* with the definite article + the noun and add *de Ud., de él, de ella, de Uds., de ellos, de ellas*:

---

su libro OR *el libro de Ud., el libro de él, el libro de ella; el libro de Uds., el libro de ellos, el libro de ellas*
sus libros OR *los libros de Ud., los libros de él, los libros de ella; los libros de Uds., los libros de ellos, los libros de ellas*

The long form is placed after the noun. The long forms are:

English Meaning	After a Singular Noun	After a Plural Noun
my; (of) mine	*mío, mía*	*míos, mías*
your; (of) yours	*tuyo, tuya*	*tuyos, tuyas*
your, his, hers, its; (of yours, of his, of hers, of its)	*suyo, suya*	*suyos, suyas*
our; (of) ours	*nuestro, nuestra*	*nuestros, nuestras*
your; (of) yours	*vuestro, vuestra*	*vuestros, vuestras*
your, their; (of yours, of theirs)	*suyo, suya*	*suyos, suyas*

Examples:
amigo mío / my friend; *un amigo mío* / a friend of mine

The long forms are used primarily:

- When you are talking directly to someone or when writing a letter to someone:

    ¡Hola, amigo mío! ¿Qué tal? / Hello, my friend! How are things?

- When you want to express "of mine," "of yours," "of his," "of hers," etc:

    Él es un amigo nuestro. / He is one of our friends.

- With the verb *ser*:

    Estos libros son míos. / These books are mine.

- In the expression:

    ¡Dios mío! / My heavens! My God!

In order to clarify the meanings of *suyo, suya, suyos, suyas* (since they are third person singular or plural), do the same as for *su* and *sus* above: *dos amigos suyos* can be clarified as: *dos amigos de Ud., dos amigos de él* (two friends of yours, of his).

The long forms of the possessive adjectives are used to serve as possessive pronouns. See §6.3, page 50.

A possessive adjective is ordinarily not used when referring to an article of clothing being worn or to parts of the body, particularly when a reflexive verb is used:

    Me lavo las manos antes de comer. / I wash my hands before eating.

§5.4–5 Interrogatives

    ¿Qué . . . ? and *¿cuál . . . ?*

- These two interrogative words both mean "what" or "which," but there is a difference in use:
- Use *¿Qué . . . ?* as a pronoun (when there is no noun right after it) if you are inquiring about something, if you want an explanation about something, or if you want something defined or described:

    ¿Qué es esto? / What is this?

- Use *¿Qué . . . ?* as an adjective when there is a noun right after it:

    ¿Qué día es hoy? / What day is it today?

- Use *¿Cuál . . . ?* as a pronoun when there is no noun right after it. If by "what" you mean "which" or "which one," it is better Spanish to use *¿Cuál . . . ?* For example:

  ¿Cuál de estos lápices es mejor? / Which (Which one) of these pencils is better?

- The same is true in the plural:

  ¿Cuáles son buenos? / Which ones are good?

- Do not use *cuál* if there is a noun right after it; in that case, you must use *qué*, as noted above.

§5.4–6   As Nouns

At times, an adjective is used as a noun if it is preceded by an article or a demonstrative adjective:

  el viejo / the old man; *aquel viejo* / that old man;
  la joven / the young lady; *estos jóvenes* / these young men;
  este ciego / this blind man

§5.5   SHORTENED FORMS

Certain masculine singular adjectives drop the final *o* when in front of a masculine singular noun:

Tip		
alguno: *algún día*	**primero:** *el primer año*
bueno: *un buen amigo*	**tercero:** *el tercer mes*
malo: *mal tiempo*	**uno:** *un dólar*
ninguno: *ningún libro*	

Note that when *alguno* and *ninguno* are shortened, an accent mark is required on the *u*.

Santo shortens to *San* before a masculine singular saint: *San Francisco, San José* but remains *Santo* in front of *Do-* or *To-*: *Santo Domingo, Santo Tomás*.

Grande shortens to *gran* when in front of any singular noun, whether masculine or feminine;

> *un gran hombre* / a great (famous) man
> *una gran mujer* / a great (famous) woman

Ciento shortens to *cien* when in front of any plural noun, whether masculine or feminine:

> *cien libros* / one (a) hundred books
> *cien sillas* / one (a) hundred chairs

Ciento shortens to *cien* except in the numbers 101 through 199:

> *cien mil* / one hundred thousand
> *ciento tres dólares* / one hundred three dollars

Note that in English we say one hundred or a hundred, but in Spanish no word is used in front of *ciento* or *cien* to express *one* or *a*; it is merely *ciento* or *cien*.

Cualquiera and *cualesquiera* lose the final *a* in front of a noun: *cualquier hombre* / any man.

§5.6 COMPARATIVES AND SUPERLATIVES

§5.6–1 Comparatives

Of equality: *tan . . . como* (as . . . as)

> *María es tan alta como Elena.* / Mary is as tall as Helen.

Of a lesser degree: *menos . . . que* (less . . . than)

> *María es menos alta que Anita.* / Mary is less tall than Anita.

Of a higher degree: *más . . . que* (more . . . than)

> *María es más alta que Isabel.* / Mary is taller than Elizabeth.

- *Tanto, tanta, tantos, tantas* + noun + *como:* as much (as many) . . . as

  > *Tengo tanto dinero como usted.* / I have as much money as you.
  > *Tengo tantos libros como usted.* / I have as many books as you.

COMPARISON BETWEEN TWO CLAUSES

- Use *de lo que* to express "than" when comparing two clauses with different verbs if an adjective or adverb is the comparison:

  Esta frase es más fácil de lo que Ud. cree. / This sentence is easier than you think.

- Use the appropriate form of *de lo que, de los que, de la que, de las que* when comparing two clauses with the same verbs if a noun is the comparison:

  Tengo más dinero de lo que Ud. tiene. / I have more money than you have.
  Roberto tiene más amigas de las que tiene Juan. / Robert has more girl friends than John has.

§5.6–2 Superlatives

- To express the superlative degree, use the comparative forms given above with the appropriate definite article:

  With a proper noun: *Anita es la más alta.* / Anita is the tallest.
  Anita y Roberto son los más altos. / Anita and Robert are the tallest.
  With a common noun: *El muchacho más alto de la clase es Roberto.* / The tallest boy in the class is Robert.

Tip	Note that after a superlative in Spanish, "in" is expressed by *de*, not *en*.

When two or more superlative adjectives describe the same noun, *más* or *menos* is used only once in front of the first adjective: *Aquella mujer es la más pobre y vieja.* / That woman is the poorest and oldest.

- Absolute superlative: adjectives ending in *-ísimo, -ísima, -ísimos, -ísimas*

To express an adjective in a very high degree, drop the final vowel (if there is one) and add the appropriate ending among the following, depending on the correct agreement: *-ísimo, -ísima, -ísimos, -ísimas:*

> *María está contentísima.* / Mary is very (extremely) happy.
> *Los muchachos están contentísimos.* / The boys are very (extremely) happy.

These forms may be used instead of *muy* + adjective:

> *una casa grandísima* / una casa muy grande

Never use *muy* in front of *mucho.* Say *muchísimo.*

> *Muchísimas gracias.* / Many thanks; thank you very, very much.

§5.6–3 Irregular Comparatives and Superlatives

Adjective	Comparative	Superlative
bueno (good)	*mejor* (better)	*el mejor* (best)
malo (bad)	*peor* (worse)	*el peor* (worst)
grande (large)	*más grande* (larger) *mayor* (greater, older)	*el más grande* (largest) *el mayor* (greatest, oldest)
pequeño (small)	*más pequeño* (smaller) *menor* (smaller, younger)	*el más pequeño* (smallest) *el menor* (smallest, youngest)

Tip	Note that you must be careful to make the correct agreement in gender and number.

- *Más que* (more than) or *menos que* (less than) becomes *más de, menos de* + a number:

  > *El señor Gómez tiene más de cincuenta años.* / Mr. Gómez is more than fifty years old.
  > BUT: *No tengo más que dos dólares.* / I have only two dollars.

  In this example, the meaning is "only," expressed by *no* in front of the verb; in this case, you must keep *que* to express "only."

- *Cuanto más (menos) . . . tanto más (menos)* / the more (the less) . . . the more (the less)

  A proportion or ratio is expressed by this phrase.

  > *Cuanto más dinero tengo, tanto más necesito.* / The more money I have, the more I need.
  > *Cuanto menos dinero tengo, tanto menos necesito.* / The less money I have, the less I need.

Tip	A note about the adjectives *poco* and *pequeño:*

These two adjectives mean "little," but note the difference.

Poco means "little" in terms of quantity:

> *Tenemos poco trabajo hoy.* / We have little work today.

Pequeño means "little" in terms of size:

> *Mi casa es pequeña.* / My house is small.

§6.

Pronouns: Beginner, Intermediate, and Advanced Levels

DEFINITION

A pronoun is a word that takes the place of a noun; for example, in English there are these common pronouns: I, you, he, she, it, we, they, me, him, her, us, them — just to mention a few. Pronouns are divided into certain types: personal, prepositional, demonstrative, possessive, relative, interrogative, indefinite, and negative.

§6.1 PERSONAL PRONOUNS

A personal pronoun is used as the subject of a verb, direct or indirect object of a verb, as a reflexive pronoun object, and as an object of a preposition.

§6.1–1 Subject Pronouns

Singular	Examples
yo / I	*Yo hablo.*
tú / you (familiar)	*Tú hablas.*
usted / you (polite)	*Usted habla.*
él / he, it	*Él habla.*
ella / she, it	*Ella habla.*

Plural	Examples
nosotros (nosotras) / we	*Nosotros hablamos.*
vosotros (vosotras) / you (fam.)	*Vosotros habláis.*
ustedes / you (polite)	*Ustedes hablan.*
ellos / they	*Ellos hablan.*
ellas / they	*Ellas hablan.*

In Spanish, subject pronouns are not used at all times. The ending of the verb tells you if the subject is 1st, 2nd, or 3rd person in the singular or plural. Of course, in the 3rd person singular and plural, there is more than one possible subject with the same ending on the verb form. In that case, if there is any doubt as to what the subject is, it is mentioned for the sake of clarity. At other times, subject pronouns in Spanish are used when you want to be emphatic, to make a contrast between this person and that person, or out of simple courtesy.

For the use of **ustedes** instead of **vosotros** and **vosotras**, see the statement at the end of **§7.5–17**.

§6.1–2 Direct Object Pronouns

Singular	Examples
me / me	*María me ha visto.* / Mary has seen me.
te / you (fam.)	*María te había visto.* / Mary had seen you.
lo, la / you (pol.)	*María lo (la) ve.* / Mary sees you.
lo / him, it	*María lo ve.* / Mary sees him (it).
la / her, it	*María la ve.* / Mary sees her (it).

Plural	Examples
nos / us	*María nos había visto.* / Mary had seen us.
os / you (fam.)	*María os ha visto.* / Mary has seen you.
los, las / you (pol.)	*María los (las) ve.* / Mary sees you.
los / them	*María los ve.* / Mary sees them.
las / them	*María las ve.* / Mary sees them.

Note that in the 3rd person plural, the direct objects *los* (m) and *las* (f) refer to people and things.

Also note that in the 3rd person singular, the direct object pronoun *lo* is masculine and *la* is feminine and both mean "you."

3rd PERSON DIRECT OBJECT PRONOUNS		
Spanish	**English**	**Gender**
lo	him, it, you	m
la	her, you, it	f
los	you (pl.), them	m
las	you (pl.), them	f

There is also the neuter *lo* direct object pronoun. It usually refers to an idea or a statement:

¿Está Ud. enfermo? / Are you sick? *Sí, lo estoy.* / Yes, I am.
¿Son amigos? / Are they friends? *Sí, lo son.* / Yes, they are.

Of course, your reply could be *Sí, estoy enfermo* and *Sí, son amigos*. But because your verb is a form of *estar* or *ser*, you do not have to repeat what was mentioned; neuter *lo* takes its place as a direct object pronoun. This neuter *lo* direct object pronoun is also used with other verbs, e.g., *pedir, preguntar,* and *parecer*:

> *María parece contenta.* / Mary seems happy.
> *Sí, lo parece.* / Yes, she does (Yes, she does seem so).

To make the examples in Spanish given above negative, place *no* in front of the direct object pronouns: *María no me ve*. To make the examples in §6.1–1 negative, place *no* in front of the verb.

§6.1–3   Indirect Object Pronouns

Singular	Examples
me / to me	*Pablo me ha hablado.* / Paul has talked to me.
te / to you (fam.)	*Pablo te habla.* / Paul talks to you.
le / to you, to him, to her, to it	*Pablo le habla.* / Paul talks to you (to him, to her, to it).
Plural	**Examples**
nos / to us	*Pablo nos ha hablado.* / Paul has talked to us.
os / to you (fam.)	*Pablo os habla.* / Paul talks to you.
les / to you, to them	*Pablo les habla.* / Paul talks to you (to them).

To make these sentences negative, place *no* in front of the indirect object pronouns:

> *Pablo no me habla.* / Paul does not talk to me.

Note that *me, te, nos, os* can be used as both direct object pronouns and indirect object pronouns.

Note that *le* as an indirect object pronoun has more than one meaning. If there is any doubt as to the meaning, merely add any of the following expressions after the verb to clarify the meaning:

> *a Ud., a él, a ella: Pablo le habla a usted.* / Paul is talking to you.

Note that *les* has more than one meaning. If there is any doubt as to the meaning, merely add any of the following expressions after the verb:

> *a Uds., a ellos, a ellas: Pablo no les habla a ellos.* / Paul is not talking to them.

As you can see in the examples given above, an indirect object pronoun ordinarily is placed in front of the main verb. Other positions are discussed later in this chapter.

An indirect object pronoun is needed when you use a verb that indicates a person is being deprived of something, e.g., to steal something from someone, to take something off or from someone, to buy something from someone, and actions of this sort. The reason an indirect object pronoun is needed is that you are dealing with the preposition *a* + noun or pronoun and it must be accounted for.

> *Los ladrones le robaron todo el dinero a él.* / The robbers stole all the money from him.
> *La madre le quitó al niño el sombrero.* / The mother took off the child's hat.

The indirect object pronouns are used with the verb *gustar* and with the following verbs: *bastar, faltar* or *hacer falta, quedarle (a uno), tocarle (a uno), placer, parecer.*

> *A Ricardo le gusta el helado.* / Richard likes ice cream (i.e., Ice cream is pleasing to him, to Richard).
> *A Juan le bastan cien dólares.* / One hundred dollars are enough for John.
> *A los muchachos les faltan cinco dólares.* / The boys need five dollars (i.e., Five dollars are lacking to them, to the boys).

OR

A la mujer le hacen falta cinco dólares. / The woman needs five
dollars (i.e., Five dollars are lacking to her, to the woman).

§6.1–4   Position of Object Pronouns

Let's review the normal position of a single object pronoun
when dealing with a simple tense or a compound tense.

Attach the single object pronoun to an infinitive:

Juan quiere escribirlo. / John wants to write it.

If the main verb is *poder, querer, saber, ir a*, you may place
the object pronoun in front of the main verb:

Juan lo quiere escribir. / John wants to write it.
¿Puedo levantarme? OR *¿Me puedo levantar?* / May I get up?

Attach the single object pronoun to a present participle:

Juan está escribiéndolo. / John is writing it.

Note that when you attach an object pronoun to a present
participle, you must add an accent mark on the vowel that
was stressed in the present participle before the object pronoun was attached.

escribiendo → *escribiéndolo*

If the main verb is a progressive form with *estar* or another
auxiliary, you may place the object pronoun in front of the
main verb:

Juan lo está escribiendo. / John is writing it.

When you are dealing with a verb form in the affirmative
imperative (command), you must attach the single object pronoun to the verb form and add an accent mark on the vowel
that was stressed in the verb form before the single object
pronoun was added.

Hable → *Hábleme*
¡Hábleme Ud., por favor! / Talk to me, please!

When you are dealing with a verb form in the negative
imperative (command), you must place the object pronoun in
front of the verb form.

¡No me hable Ud., por favor! / Do not talk to me, please!

§6.1–5 Position of Double Object Pronouns: A Summary

An indirect object pronoun is always placed in front of a direct object pronoun.

Tip

With a verb in a simple tense or in a compound tense in the affirmative or negative:

The indirect object pronoun is placed in front of the direct object pronoun and both are placed in front of the verb form.

Juan me lo da. / John is giving it to me.
Juan nos los dio. / John gave them to us.
María no me lo ha dado. / Mary has not given it to me.

Tip

With a verb in a simple tense or in a compound tense in the interrogative:

The indirect object pronoun remains in front of the direct object pronoun and both remain in front of the verb form. The subject (whether a noun or pronoun) is placed after the verb form.

¿Nos la dio Juan? / Did John give it to us?

Tip

With a verb in the affirmative imperative (command):

The object pronouns are still in the same order (indirect object + direct object) but they are attached to the verb form and an accent mark is added on the vowel that was stressed in the verb form before the two object pronouns were added.

¡Dígamelo Ud., por favor! / Tell it to me, please!

Tip

With a verb in the negative imperative (command):

The position of *no* and the two object pronouns is the same as usual, in front of the verb form.

¡No me lo diga Ud., por favor! / Don't tell it to me, please!

Tip

When dealing with an infinitive, attach both object pronouns (indirect, direct) to the infinitive.

Juan quiere dármelo. / John wants to give it to me.

OR

If the main verb is *poder, querer, saber, ir a*, you may place the two object pronouns in front of the main verb.

Juan me lo quiere dar. / John wants to give it to me.

Tip

When dealing with a present participle, attach both object pronouns (indirect, direct) to the present participle:

Juan está escribiéndomelo. / John is writing it to me.

OR

If the main verb is a progressive form with *estar* or another auxiliary, you may place the two object pronouns (indirect, direct) in front of the main verb:

Juan me lo está escribiendo. / John is writing it to me.
Juana me lo estaba escribiendo. / Jane was writing it to me.

Tip

When an indirect object pronoun and a direct object pronoun are both 3rd person, the indirect object pronoun (*le* or *les*) changes to *se* because it cannot stand as *le* or *les* in front of a direct object pronoun beginning with the letter "l."

Juan se lo da. / John is giving it to you (to him, to her, to it, to you [plural], to them).

¡Dígaselo Ud.! / Tell it to him!

¡No se lo diga Ud.! / Don't tell it to him!

Juan quiere dárselo.
Juan se lo quiere dar. } John wants to give it to her.

Juan está escribiéndoselo. } John is writing it to
Juan se lo está escribiendo. } them.

Since the form *se* can have more than one meaning (to him, to her, to them, etc.), in addition to the fact that it looks exactly like the reflexive pronoun *se,* any doubt as to its meaning can be clarified merely by adding any of the following accordingly: *a Ud., a él, a ella, a Uds., a ellos, a ellas.*

Juan se lo da a ella. / John is giving it to her.

Tip

When you are dealing with double object pronouns (one direct and the other indirect), remember that people are more important than things; therefore, the indirect object pronoun (usually referring to a person) goes in front of the direct object pronoun (usually referring to a thing).

María está escribiendo el mensaje de texto a Pablo. / Mary is writing the text message to Paul.

María se lo está escribiendo. / Mary is writing it to him. (*se* = *a Pablo*; *lo* = *el mensaje de texto*)

§6.1–6 Reflexive Pronouns

Singular	Examples
me / myself	*Me lavo.* / I wash myself.
te / yourself	*Te lavas.* / You wash yourself.
se / yourself, himself, herself, itself	*Ud. se lava.* / You wash yourself; *Pablo se lava.* / Paul washes himself, etc.

Plural	Examples
nos / ourselves	*Nosotros (-as) nos lavamos.* / We wash ourselves.
os / yourselves	*Vosotros (-as) os laváis.* / You wash yourselves.
se / yourselves, themselves	*Uds. se lavan.* / You wash yourselves. *Ellos (Ellas) se lavan.* / They wash themselves.

A reflexive verb contains a reflexive pronoun, and the action of the verb falls on the subject and its reflexive pronoun either directly or indirectly. For that reason the reflexive pronoun must agree with the subject: *yo me . . . , tú te . . . , Ud. se . . . , él se . . . , ella se . . . , nosotros nos . . . , vosotros os . . . , Uds. se . . . , ellos se . . . , ellas se . . . .*

A reflexive pronoun is ordinarily placed in front of the verb form, as you can see in the examples given above.

To make these sentences negative, place *no* in front of the reflexive pronoun: *Yo no me lavo, Tú no te lavas, Ud. no se lava*, etc.

Note that *me, te, nos, os* are not only reflexive pronouns

but they are also direct object pronouns and indirect object pronouns.

A reflexive verb in Spanish is not always reflexive in English.

Spanish	English
levantarse	to get up
sentarse	to sit down

There are some reflexive verbs in Spanish that are also reflexive in English.

Spanish	English
bañarse	to bathe oneself
lavarse	to wash oneself

The following reflexive pronouns are also used as reciprocal pronouns, meaning "each other" or "to each other": *se, nos, os.*

> *Ayer por la noche, María y yo nos vimos en el cine.* / Yesterday evening, Mary and I saw each other at the movies.
> *Roberto y Teresa se escriben todos los días.* / Robert and Teresa write to each other every day.

If the meaning of these three reflexive pronouns is not clear when they are used in a reciprocal meaning, any of the following may be added accordingly to express the idea of "each other" or "to each other": *uno a otro, una a otra, unos a otros,* etc.

If you are dealing with a reflexive pronoun, it is normally placed in front of an object pronoun.

The sentence

> *Yo me puse el sombrero.* / I put on my hat.

can be shortened to

> *Yo me lo puse.* / I put it on (me, on myself).

§6.1–7 Prepositional Pronouns

Pronouns that are used as objects of prepositions are called prepositional pronouns or disjunctive pronouns. They are:

Singular	Plural
para mí / for me, for myself	*para nosotros (nosotras)* / for us, for ourselves
para ti / for you, for yourself	*para vosotros (vosotras)* / for you, for yourselves
para usted (Ud.) / for you	*para ustedes (Uds.)* / for you
para él / for him, for it	*para ellos* / for them
para ella / for her, for it	*para ellas* / for them

Note the following exceptions with the prepositions *con*, *entre*, and *menos*:

conmigo / with me *entre tú y yo* / between you and me
contigo / with you (fam.) *menos yo* / except me
consigo / with yourself, with yourselves, with himself, with herself, with themselves
¿Quisieras ir al cine conmigo? / Would you like to go to the movies with me?

§6.2 DEMONSTRATIVE PRONOUNS

Demonstrative pronouns are formed from the demonstrative adjectives. To form a demonstrative pronoun write an accent mark on the stressed vowel of a demonstrative adjective. A demonstrative pronoun takes the place of a noun. It agrees in gender and number with the noun it replaces. The demonstrative pronouns are:

Masculine	Feminine	Neuter	English Meaning
éste	*ésta*	*esto*	this one (here)
éstos	*éstas*		these (here)
ése	*ésa*	*eso*	that one (there)
ésos	*ésas*		those (there)
aquél	*aquélla*	*aquello*	that one ⎱ (farther away or
aquéllos	*aquéllas*		those ⎰ out of sight)

Examples:

Me gustan este cuadro y ése. / I like this picture and that one.
Estas camisas y aquéllas son hermosas. / These shirts and those are beautiful.

> **Tip**
>
> To help you remember that a demonstrative pronoun is formed from a demonstrative adjective, you can look at the written accent mark (') over the stressed vowel in the demonstrative pronoun as a marker that makes the word stand alone as a pronoun. As such, there is no noun after it: *éste* / this one. However, there is a noun after the demonstrative adjective: *este libro* / this book.

§6.2–1 Neuter Forms

Note that the neuter forms do not have an accent mark. They are not used when you are referring to a particular noun. They are used when referring to an idea, a statement, a situation, a clause, or a phrase. Never use the neuter pronouns to refer to a person.

¿Qué es esto? / What is this?
Eso es fácil de hacer. / That is easy to do.
Juan no estudia y esto me inquieta. / John does not study and this worries me.

Note also that the English term "the latter" is expressed in Spanish as *éste, ésta, éstos,* or *éstas*; and "the former" is expressed in Spanish as *aquél, aquélla, aquéllos, aquéllas* — depending on the gender and number of the noun referred to.

> *Tengo dos hermanos, Orlando y Jaime. Aquél es autor y éste es crítico. ¡No se entienden bien!* / I have two brothers, Roland and James. The former is an author, and the latter is a critic. They don't get along well with each other!

The pronouns *el de, la de, los de, las de; el que, la que, los que, las que* are used in place of nouns.

Examples:

mi hermano y el (hermano) de mi amigo / my brother and my friend's
mi hermana y la (hermana) de mi amigo / my sister and my friend's
mis hermanos y los (hermanos) del muchacho / my brothers and the boy's
El (muchacho) que baila con María es mi hermano. / The one (boy) who is dancing with Mary is my brother.
La (muchacha) que baila con Roberto es mi hermana. / The one (girl) who is dancing with Robert is my sister.
Las (muchachas) que bailan son mis amigas. / The ones (girls) who are dancing are my friends.

§6.3 POSSESSIVE PRONOUNS

A possessive pronoun is a word that takes the place of a noun to show possession, as in English: mine, yours, etc.

You form a possessive pronoun by using the appropriate definite article (*el, la, los, las*) + the long form of the possessive adjective. A possessive pronoun agrees in gender and number with the noun it replaces. It does not agree with the possessor.

The possessive pronouns are:

English Meaning	Singular Form	Plural Form
	(agrees in gender and number with the noun it replaces)	(agrees in gender and number with the noun it replaces)
mine	el mío, la mía	los míos, las mías
yours (fam. sing.)	el tuyo, la tuya	los tuyos, las tuyas
yours, his, hers, its	el suyo, la suya	los suyos, las suyas
ours	el nuestro, la nuestra	los nuestros, las nuestras
yours (fam. pl.)	el vuestro, la vuestra	los vuestros, las vuestras
yours, theirs	el suyo, la suya	los suyos, las suyas

Examples:

Mi hermano es más alto que el suyo. / My brother is taller than yours (his, hers, theirs).

Su hermana es más alta que la mía. / Your sister is taller than mine.

In order to clarify the meanings of *el suyo, la suya, los suyos, las suyas* (since they can mean yours, his, hers, its, theirs), drop the *suyo* form, keep the appropriate definite article (*el, la, los, las*), and add any of the following: *de Ud., de él, de ella, de Uds., de ellos, de ellas.*

> *mi libro y el de Ud., mi casa y la de él, mis amigos y los de ella, mis amigas y las de Uds.* / my book and yours, my house and his, my friends and hers, my friends and yours, etc.

§6.3–1   *¿De quién es . . . ?*

"Whose," when asking a question (usually at the beginning of a sentence), is expressed by *¿De quién es...?* or *¿De quiénes es...?* If you believe that the possessor is singular, use *¿De*

quién es . . . ? If you think that the possessor is plural, use
¿De quiénes es . . . ? And if the noun you have in mind (whose
. . .) is plural, use the third person plural form of *ser:*

¿De quién es esta casa? / Whose house is this?
Es de mi tío. / It is my uncle's.
¿De quiénes es esta casa? / Whose house is this?
Es de mis amigos. / It is my friends'.
¿De quién son estos guantes? / Whose gloves are these?
Son de Juan. / They are John's.
¿De quiénes son estos niños? / Whose children are these?
Son de los señores Pardo. / They are Mr. and Mrs.
  Pardo's.

Note that the verb *ser* is used in these expressions showing
possession.

Also note that if a possessive pronoun is used with the
verb *ser,* the definite article is dropped:

¿De quién es este lápiz? / Whose pencil is this?
Es mío. / It is mine.
¿De quién son estas camisas? / Whose shirts are these?
Son suyas. / They are theirs (yours, his, hers).

OR,

Son de Ud., Son de él, Son de ella. / They are yours, They
  are his, They are hers.

---

§6.4 RELATIVE PRONOUNS

A pronoun is a word that takes the place of a noun. A relative
pronoun is a pronoun that refers to an antecedent. An
antecedent is something that comes before something; it can
be a word, a phrase, or a clause that is replaced by a pronoun

or some other substitute. **Example:** "Is it Mary who did that?" In this sentence, "who" is the relative pronoun and "Mary" is the antecedent.

In Spanish, a relative pronoun can refer to an antecedent that is a person or a thing, or an idea. A relative pronoun can be the subject or object of a verb, or the object of a preposition.

§6.4–1 *Que*

The relative pronoun *que* can mean who, that, whom, or which. It is used in the following ways:

- As the subject referring to a person:

    La muchacha que habla con Juan es mi hermana. / The girl who is talking with John is my sister.

    The relative pronoun *que* is the subject of the verb *habla* and refers to *la muchacha*, which is the subject of *es*.

- As the subject referring to a thing:

    El libro que está en la mesa es mío. / The book which (that) is on the table is mine.

    The relative pronoun *que* is the subject of the verb *está* and refers to *el libro*, which is the subject of *es*.

- As the direct object of a verb referring to a person:

    El señor Molina es el profesor que admiro. / Mr. Molina is the professor whom I admire.

    The relative pronoun *que* is the object of the verb form *admiro*. It refers to *el profesor*.

- As the direct object of a verb referring to a thing:

    La composición que Ud. lee es mía. / The composition (that, which) you are reading is mine.

    Note, in the English translation of this example, that we do not always use a relative pronoun in English. In Spanish, it must be stated.

• As the object of a preposition referring only to a thing:

> *La cama en que duermo es grande.* / The bed in which I sleep is large.

The relative pronoun *que* is the object of the preposition *en*. It refers to *la cama*. Other prepositions used commonly with *que* are *a*, *con*, *de*.

• As the object of a preposition, *que* refers to a thing only — not to a person. Use *quien* or *quienes* as the object of a preposition referring to persons.

§6.4–2 *Quien*

The relative pronoun *quien* means who or whom. It is used in the following ways:

• As the subject of a verb referring only to persons:

> *Yo sé quien lo hizo.* / I know who did it.

Quien is the subject of *hizo*. It does not refer to a specific antecedent. Here, *quien* includes its antecedent.

When used as a subject, *quien* (or *quienes*, if plural) can also mean he who, she who, the one who, the ones who, those who. In place of *quien* or *quienes* in this sense, you can also use *el que*, *la que*, *los que*, *las que*.

Tip	
	Quien escucha oye. / Who listens hears. He who listens hears. She who listens hears.
	OR:
	El que escucha oye. / He who listens hears. *La que escucha oye.* / She who listens hears. *Quienes escuchan oyen.* / Those who listen hear. The ones who listen hear.
	OR:
	Los que escuchan oyen. Las que escuchan oyen. / Those who listen hear.

- As the subject of a verb, the relative pronoun *quien* may be used instead of *que* referring only to persons when it is the subject of a nonrestrictive dependent clause set off by commas:

    La señora Gómez, quien (or que) es profesora, conoce a mi madre. / Mrs. Gómez, who is a teacher, knows my mother.

- As the direct object of a verb referring only to persons, the relative pronoun *quien* or *quienes* may be used with the personal *a* (*a quien, a quienes*) instead of *que*:

    La muchacha que (or a quien) Ud. vio en el baile es mi hermana. / The girl whom you saw at the dance is my sister.

- As the object of a preposition referring only to persons:

    ¿Conoces a la chica con quien tomé el almuerzo? / Do you know the girl with whom I had lunch?
    ¿Conoces a los chicos con quienes María tomó el almuerzo? / Do you know the boys with whom Mary had lunch?
    ¿Conoce Ud. a los hombres de quienes hablo? / Do you know the men of whom (about whom) I am talking?

§6.4–3 *el cual, la cual, los cuales, las cuales* / who, that, whom, which, the one which (that), the ones which (that), the one who, the ones who

These relative pronouns may be used in place of *que* to clarify the gender and number of *que*:

La madre de José, la cual es muy inteligente, es dentista. / Joseph's mother, who is very intelligent, is a dentist.

These substitute relative pronouns may also refer to things:

El libro, el cual está sobre la mesa, es mío. / The book, which is on the table, is mine.

These relative pronouns are also used as substitutes for *el que, la que, los que, las que* when used as the subject of a nonrestrictive dependent clause set off by commas:

*La señora Gómez, la cual (or la que, or quien, or que) es profeso-
ra, conoce a mi madre.* / Mrs. Gómez, who is a teacher, knows
my mother.

These relative pronouns, as well as *el que, la que, los que,
las que*, are used as objects of prepositions except with *a,
con, de, en* — in which case the relative pronoun *que* is pre-
ferred with things. These relative pronouns (*el cual, la cual, los
cuales, las cuales* and *el que, la que, los que, las que*) are
commonly used with the following prepositions: *para, por, sin,
delante de, cerca de*, and *sobre*:

*En este cuarto, hay una gran ventana por la cual se ve el sol por
la mañana.* / In this room, there is a large window through
which you (one, anyone) can see the sun in the morning.

These compound relative pronouns refer to persons as
well as things and can be used as the subject of a verb or the
direct object of a verb when used in a nonrestrictive dependent clause separated from its antecedent and set off with
commas.

§6.4–4   *lo cual* / which; *lo que* / what, that which

These are neuter compound relative pronouns. They do not
refer to an antecedent of any gender or number.

Lo cual and *lo que* refer to a statement, a clause, an idea:

*Mi hijo Juan estudia sus lecciones todos los días, lo cual es
bueno.* / My son John studies his lessons every day, which is
good.

Mi hija recibió buenas notas, lo que me gustó. / My daughter
received good grades, which pleased me.

Lo que is also used to express "what" in the sense of "that
which":

Comprendo lo que Ud. dice. / I understand what (that which) you
say.

Lo que Ud. dice es verdad. / What (That which) you say is true.

§6.4–5 *cuanto = todo lo que* / all that

As a relative pronoun, *cuanto* may be used in place of *todo lo que*:

> *Todo lo que Ud. dice es verdad;*

OR

> *Cuanto Ud. dice es verdad.* / All that (All that which) you say is
> true.

§6.4–6 *cuyo, cuya, cuyos, cuyas* / whose

This word (and its forms as given) refers to persons and
things. Strictly speaking, *cuyo*, etc. is not regarded as a relative pronoun but rather as a relative possessive adjective. It
agrees in gender and number with what is possessed (whose
. . .), not with the possessor. Its position is directly in front of
the noun it modifies.

> *El señor García, cuyos hijos son inteligentes, es profesor.* / Mr.
> García, whose children are intelligent, is a professor.
> *El muchacho, cuya madre es profesora, es inteligente.* / The boy,
> whose mother is a professor, is intelligent.

Tip	The forms of *cuyo* cannot be used as an interrogative when you ask "Whose is . . . ?" You must use *de quién*: ¿De quién es este libro?

When referring to parts of the body, use *a quien* instead of
cuyo:

> *La niña, a quien la madre lavó las manos, es bonita.* / The girl,
> whose hands the mother washed, is pretty.

§6.5 INTERROGATIVE PRONOUNS

See also specific interrogatives (*qué, cuál,* etc.) in the index.
Here are a few common interrogatives that you should be

aware of. Note the required accent mark on these words when used in a question.

¿*qué* . . . ? / what . . . ?
¿*cuál* . . . ? / which, which one . . . ?
¿*cuáles* . . . ? / which, which ones . . . ?
¿*quién* . . . ? ¿*quiénes* . . . ? / who . . . ?
¿*a quién* . . . ? ¿*a quiénes* . . . ? / whom . . . ? to whom . . . ?
¿*de quién* . . . ? / of whom, from whom, by whom,
  whose . . . ?
¿*De quién es este lápiz?* / Whose pencil is this?

---

§6.6 INDEFINITE PRONOUNS

algo / something, anything
(with *sin,* use *nada*: *sin nada* / without anything)
alguien / anybody, anyone, someone, somebody
(with *sin,* use *nadie*: *sin nadie* / without anyone)
alguno, alguna, algunos, algunas / some, any

§6.7 NEGATIVE PRONOUNS

nada / nothing: *sin nada* / without anything
(after *sin*, *nada* is used instead of *algo*: *Ella no quiere nada* / She
  does not want anything.)
nadie / nobody, no one, not anyone, not anybody: sin *nadie* /
  without anybody
(after *sin*, *nadie* is used instead of *alguien*)
ninguno, ninguna / no one, none, not any, not anybody

§7.

Verbs: Beginner, Intermediate, and Advanced Levels

For a summary of the names of verb tenses and moods, see page 132.

§7.1   AGREEMENT

§7.1–1   Subject and Verb

A subject and verb form must agree in person (1st, 2nd, or 3rd) and number (singular or plural). To get a picture of the three persons in the singular and in the plural, see subject pronouns in §6.

§7.1–2   Subject and Reflexive Pronoun of a Reflexive Verb

A subject and reflexive pronoun must agree in person and number. To get a picture of the correct reflexive pronoun that goes with the subject, according to the person you need (1st, 2nd, or 3rd, singular or plural), see reflexive pronouns in §6.1–6.

§7.2   TYPES

§7.2–1   Auxiliary (helping) Verb *haber* (to have)

The auxiliary (helping) verb *haber* is used in any of the seven simple tenses + the past participle of the main verb to form the seven compound tenses. Please read §7.5-19 to see *haber* conjugated in the seven simple tenses.

§7.2–2   Transitive Verbs

A transitive verb is a verb that takes a direct object. It is transitive because the action passes over from the subject and directly affects someone or something in some way.

> *Veo a mi amigo.* / I see my friend.
> *Abro la ventana.* / I open the window.

When the direct object of the verb is a pronoun, it is placed in front of the verb most of the time; at other times it is attached to an infinitive; if the main verb is *poder, querer, saber, ir a +* infinitive, the direct object pronoun may be placed in front of the main verb instead of attaching it to the infinitive; at other times, the direct object pronoun is attached to a present participle. For an in-depth analysis of the word order of elements in Spanish sentences, particularly pronouns, review §6.

Here are the same sentences as above, but with direct object pronouns instead of direct object nouns:

> *(Yo) lo veo.* / I see him.
> *(Yo) la abro.* / I open it.

For the position of pronouns in other types of sentences in Spanish, review position of object pronouns in §6.

§7.2–3   Intransitive Verbs

An intransitive verb is a verb that does not take a direct object. It is called intransitive because the action does not pass over from the subject and directly affect anyone or anything.

> *La profesora está hablando.* / The teacher is talking.
> *La señora Gómez salió temprano.* / Mrs. Gómez left early.

An intransitive verb takes an indirect object.

> *La profesora está hablando a los alumnos.* / The teacher is talking to the students.

The indirect object noun is *alumnos* because it is preceded by *a los* (to the).

> *La profesora les está hablando.* / The teacher is talking to them.

The indirect object is the pronoun *les*, to them.

For a review of direct object pronouns and indirect object pronouns, see §6.

A transitive verb can take an indirect object.

> *La profesora da los libros a los alumnos.* / The teacher is giving the books to the pupils.

The direct object is *los libros*; the indirect object is *a los alumnos*.

> *La profesora los da a los alumnos.* / The teacher is giving them to the pupils.

The direct object pronoun is *los* (meaning *los libros*) and the indirect object is still *a los alumnos*.

> *La profesora les da los libros.* / The teacher is giving the books to them.

The indirect object pronoun is *les* (meaning "to them," i.e., *a los alumnos*).

> *La profesora se los da.* / The teacher is giving them to them.

The indirect object pronoun *les* changes to *se* because *les* is 3rd person and it is followed by *los*, a direct object pronoun, which is also 3rd person. For a review of this point in Spanish grammar, see position of double object pronouns in §6.

You may clarify the indirect object pronoun *se* in this sentence by adding *a ellos* or *a los alumnos*.

> *La profesora se los da a ellos.* / The teacher is giving them to them.

§7.3 PARTICIPLES

§7.3–1 Past Participle

A past participle is regularly formed as follows:

Infinitive	Drop	Add	To the Stem	You Get
trabajar	*-ar*	*ado*	*trabaj*	*trabajado*
comer	*-er*	*ido*	*com*	*comido*
recibir	*-ir*	*ido*	*recib*	*recibido*

COMMON IRREGULAR PAST PARTICIPLES

Infinitive	Past Participle
abrir / to open	*abierto* / opened
caer / to fall	*caído* / fallen
creer / to believe	*creído* / believed
cubrir / to cover	*cubierto* / covered
decir / to say, to tell	*dicho* / said, told
devolver / to return (something)	*devuelto* / returned (something)
escribir / to write	*escrito* / written
hacer / to do, to make	*hecho* / done, made
ir / to go	*ido* / gone
leer / to read	*leído* / read
morir / to die	*muerto* / died
oír / to hear	*oído* / heard
poner / to put	*puesto* / put
reír / to laugh	*reído* / laughed
resolver / to resolve, to solve	*resuelto* / resolved, solved
romper / to break	*roto* / broken
traer / to bring	*traído* / brought
ver / to see	*visto* / seen
volver / to return	*vuelto* / returned

Uses of the Past Participle

To form the compound tenses:

As in English, the past participle is needed to form the compound tenses in Spanish, of which there are seven. For the complete conjugation showing the forms of the six persons in each of the following compound tenses and for an explanation of how they are formed, see the specific name of each tense in the index.

THE COMPOUND TENSES	
Name of tense	**Example (1st person, singular)**
Present Perfect Indicative	*he hablado*
Pluperfect Indicative	*había hablado*
Preterit Perfect	*hube hablado*
Future Perfect	*habré hablado*
Conditional Perfect	*habría hablado*
Present Perfect Subjunctive	*haya hablado*
Pluperfect Subjunctive	*hubiera hablado* or *hubiese hablado*

Other Uses of the Past Participle

To form the Perfect Infinitive:

haber hablado / to have spoken

To form the Perfect Participle:

habiendo hablado / having spoken

To serve as an adjective, which must agree in gender and number with the noun it modifies:

El señor Molina es muy respetado. / Mr. Molina is very respected.

La señora González es muy conocida. / Mrs. González is very well known.

To express the result of an action with *estar*:

La puerta está abierta. / The door is open.
Las cartas están escritas. / The letters are written.

To express the passive voice with *ser*:

La ventana fue abierta por el ladrón. / The window was opened by the robber.

§7.3–2 Present Participle (*gerundio*)

A present participle is a verb form which, in English, ends in -ing: singing, eating, receiving. In Spanish, a present participle is regularly formed as follows:

---

drop the *ar* of an *-ar* ending verb, like *cantar*, and add
  -ando: cantando / singing
drop the *er* of an *-er* ending verb, like *comer*, and add
  -iendo: comiendo / eating
drop the *ir* of an *-ir* ending verb, like *recibir*, and add
  -iendo: recibiendo / receiving

Gerunds and Present Participles

In English, a gerund also ends in -ing but there is a distinct difference in use between a gerund and a present participle. When a present participle is used as a noun it is called a gerund; for example: Reading is good. As a present participle: The boy fell asleep while reading.

In the first example (Reading is good), reading is a gerund because it is the subject of the verb "is." In Spanish, however, we must not use the present participle form as a noun to serve as a subject; we must use the infinitive form of the verb: *Leer es bueno.*

COMMON IRREGULAR PRESENT PARTICIPLES

Infinitive

Present Participle

caer / to fall

cayendo / falling

construir / to construct

construyendo / constructing

corregir / to correct

corrigiendo / correcting

creer / to believe

creyendo / believing

decir / to say, to tell

diciendo / saying, telling

despedirse / to say good-bye

despidiéndose / saying good-bye

divertirse / to enjoy oneself

divirtiéndose / enjoying oneself

dormir / to sleep

durmiendo / sleeping

ir / to go

yendo / going

leer / to read

leyendo / reading

mentir / to lie (tell a falsehood)

mintiendo / lying

morir / to die

muriendo / dying

oír / to hear

oyendo / hearing

pedir / to ask (for), to request

pidiendo /asking (for), requesting

poder / to be able

pudiendo / being able

reír / to laugh

riendo / laughing

repetir / to repeat

repitiendo / repeating

seguir / to follow

siguiendo / following

sentir / to feel

sintiendo / feeling

servir / to serve

sirviendo / serving

traer / to bring

trayendo / bringing

venir / to come

viniendo / coming

vestir / to dress

vistiendo / dressing

Uses of the Present Participle

To form the progressive tenses:

The progressive present is commonly formed by using *estar* in the present tense plus the present participle of the main verb you are using.

Estoy hablando. / I am talking.

The progressive past is commonly formed by using *estar* in the imperfect indicative plus the present participle of the main verb you are using.

Estaba hablando. / I was talking.

Instead of using *estar*, as noted above, to form these two progressive tenses, sometimes *ir* (to go), *seguir* (to follow, to continue), *continuar* (to continue) can be used.

Examples:

Va hablando. / He (she) keeps right on talking.
Iba hablando. / He (she) kept right on talking.
Siga leyendo, por favor. / Keep on reading, please.
María continúa divirtiéndose. / Mary continues enjoying herself.

To express vividly an action that occurred (preterit + present participle):

El niño entró llorando en la casa. / The little boy came into the house crying.

To express the English use of "by" + present participle in Spanish, we use the gerund form, which has the same ending as a present participle.

Trabajando se gana dinero. / By working, one earns (a person earns) money.
Estudiando mucho, Pepe recibió buenas notas. / By studying hard, Joe received good grades.

No preposition is used in front of the present participle (the Spanish gerund) even though it is expressed in English as "by" + present participle.

In Spanish we use *al* + infinitive (not + present participle) to express "on" or "upon" + present participle:

Al entrar en la casa, el niño comenzó a llorar. / Upon entering the house, the little boy began to cry.

To form the perfect participle:

habiendo hablado / having talked

§7.4 VERBS AND PREPOSITIONS

In this section you will learn what preposition goes with what verb.

A verb right after a preposition is in the infinitive form:

Pablo salió sin hablar. / Paul went out without talking.

§7.4–1 Verbs of Motion That Take the Preposition *a* + Infinitive

ir a / to go to
regresar a / to return to
salir a / to go out to
venir a / to come to
volver a / to return to

Example:

María fue a comer. / Mary went to eat.

§7.4–2 Verbs That Take the Preposition *a* + Infinitive

aprender a / to learn to, to learn how to
aspirar a / to aspire to
ayudar a (hacer algo) / to help to
comenzar a / to begin to
decidirse a / to decide to
dedicarse a / to devote oneself to
detenerse a / to pause to, to stop to
empezar a / to begin to, to start to
enseñar a / to teach to

invitar a / to invite to
negarse a / to refuse to
ponerse a / to begin to, to start to
prepararse a / to prepare (oneself) to
principiar a / to begin to, to start to
venir a / to end up by
volver a / to do something again

Examples:

> *El señor Gómez se negó a ir.* / Mr. Gómez refused to go.
> *Juana se puso a correr.* / Jane began to run.
> *El muchacho volvió a jugar.* / The boy played again.

§7.4–3 Verbs That Take the Preposition *a* + Noun (or Pronoun)

acercarse a / to approach
asistir a / to attend, to be present at
asomarse a / to appear at
dar a / to face, to overlook, to look out upon, to look out over
dedicarse a / to devote oneself to
echar una carta al correo / to mail, to post a letter
jugar a / to play (a game, sport, cards)
llegar a ser / to become
querer a / to love
ser aficionado a / to be fond of, to be a fan of
subir a / to get on, to get into (a bus, a train, a vehicle)

Examples:

> *Nos acercamos a la ciudad.* / We are approaching the city.
> *Una muchacha bonita se asomó a la puerta.* / A pretty girl
>   appeared at the door.
> *Mi cuarto da al jardín.* / My room faces the garden.
> *Me dedico a mis estudios.* / I devote myself to my studies.

§7.4–4 Verbs That Take the Preposition *con* + Infinitive

contar con / to count on, to rely on
soñar con / to dream of, to dream about

Examples:

Cuento con tener éxito. / I am counting on being successful.
Sueño con ir a Chile. / I dream of going to Chile.

§7.4–5 Verbs That Take the Preposition *con* + Noun (or Pronoun)

casarse con / to marry, to get married to
cumplir con / to fulfill
dar con / to meet, to find, to come upon
encontrarse con / to run into, to meet by chance

Example:

José se casó con Ana. / Joseph married Anna.

§7.4–6 Verbs That Take the Preposition *de* + Infinitive

acabar de / to have just
acordarse de / to remember to
alegrarse de / to be glad to
cansarse de / to become tired of
dejar de / to stop, to fail to
ocuparse de / to be busy with, to attend to
olvidarse de / to forget to
tratar de / to try to

Examples:

> *Guillermo acaba de llegar.* / William has just arrived.
> *Me alegro de hablarle.* / I am glad to talk to you.
> *Me canso de esperar el autobús.* / I'm getting tired of
>   waiting for the bus.

§7.4–7   Verbs That Take the Preposition *de* +
Noun (or Pronoun)

acordarse de / to remember
aprovecharse de / to take advantage of
bajar de / to get out of, to descend from, to get off
burlarse de / to make fun of
cambiar de / to change (trains, buses, clothes, etc.)
cansarse de / to become tired of

Examples:

> *Me acuerdo de aquel hombre.* / I remember that man.
> *Vamos a aprovecharnos de esta oportunidad.* / Let's take
>   advantage of this opportunity.
> *Después de bajar del tren, fui a comer.* / After getting off
>   the train, I went to eat.
> *Todos los días cambio de ropa.* / Every day I change my
>   clothes.
> *Me canso de este trabajo.* / I am getting tired of this work.

§7.4–8   Verbs That Generally Take the
Preposition *en* + Infinitive

consentir en / to consent to
convenir en / to agree to, to agree on

empeñarse en / to persist in, to insist on
insistir en / to insist on
quedar en / to agree to, to agree on
tardar en / to be late (to delay) in

Examples:

> *El muchacho se empeñó en salir.* / The boy insisted on going out.
> *El avión tardó en llegar.* / The plane was late in arriving.

§7.4–9 Verbs That Generally Take the Preposition *en* + Noun (or Pronoun)

apoyarse en / to lean against, to lean on
confiar en / to rely on, to trust in
consistir en / to consist of
entrar en / to enter (into), to go into
fijarse en / to stare at, to notice, to take notice, to observe
pensar en / to think of, to think about (*pensar en* is used when asking or when stating what or whom a person is thinking of)
ponerse en camino / to set out, to start out

Examples:

> *Me apoyé en la puerta.* / I leaned against the door.
> *Entré en el restaurante.* / I entered (I went in) the restaurant.

> *¿En qué piensa Ud.?* / What are you thinking of?
> *Pienso en mi trabajo.* / I am thinking of my work.

§7.4–10 Verbs That Generally Take the Preposition *por* + Infinitive, Noun, Pronoun, Adjective

acabar por / to end up by
dar por / to consider, to regard as
darse por / to pretend (to be something), to think oneself (to be something)
estar por / to be in favor of
interesarse por / to take an interest in
preguntar por / to ask for, to inquire about

Examples:

Domingo acabó por casarse con Elena. / Dominic finally ended up by marrying Helen.
¿Mi libro de español? Lo doy por perdido. / My Spanish book? I consider it lost.
La señorita López se da por actriz. / Miss López pretends to be an actress.

§7.4–11 Verb + no Preposition + Infinitive

deber + infinitive / must, ought to

Debo hacer mis lecciones. / I must (ought to) do my lessons.

Verbs That Do Not Ordinarily Take a Preposition When Followed by an Infinitive

decidir + infinitive / to decide
dejar + infinitive / to allow to, to let

Mi madre me dejó salir. / My mother allowed me to go out.
Dejé caer mi libro. / I dropped my book (I let my book fall).

desear + infinitive / to desire to, to wish to

Deseo tomar un café. / I wish to have a cup of coffee.

esperar + infinitive / to expect to, to hope to

Espero ir a la América del Sur este invierno. / I expect to
go to South America this winter.

hacer + infinitive / to do, to make, to have something made or
done

Tú me haces reír. / You make me laugh.

necesitar + infinitive / to need

Necesito pasar una hora en la biblioteca. / I need to spend
an hour in the library.

oír + infinitive / to hear

Le oí entrar por la ventana. / I heard him enter through the
window.

pensar + infinitive / to intend to, to plan to

Pienso hacer un viaje a México. / I plan to take a trip to Mexico.

poder + infinitive / to be able to, can

Puedo venir a verle a la una. / I can come to see you at one o'clock.

preferir + infinitive / to prefer

Prefiero quedarme en casa esta noche. / I prefer to stay at home this evening.

prometer + infinitive / to promise

Prometo venir a verle a las ocho. / I promise to come to see you at eight o'clock.

querer + infinitive / to want to, to wish to

Quiero comer ahora. / I want to eat now.

saber + infinitive / to know how to

¿Sabe Ud. nadar? / Do you know how to swim?
Sí, yo sé nadar. / Yes, I know how to swim.

ver + infinitive / to see

> *Veo venir el tren.* / I see the train coming.

§7.4–12 Verbs That Do Not Ordinarily Require a Preposition, Whereas in English a Preposition Is Used

Many English phrasal verbs (verbs with a preposition) do not need a preposition to express the same thought in Spanish.

buscar / to look for, to search for

> *Busco mi libro.* / I am looking for my book.

escuchar / to listen to

> *Escucho la música.* / I am listening to the music.

esperar / to wait for

> *Espero el autobús.* / I am waiting for the bus.

guardar cama / to stay in bed

> *La semana pasada guardé cama porque estaba enfermo.* / Last week I stayed in bed because I was sick.

mirar / to look at

> *Miro el cielo.* / I am looking at the sky.

pagar / to pay for

> *Pagué los billetes.* / I paid for the tickets.

pedir / to ask for

> *Pido un libro.* / I am asking for a book.

§7.5 TENSES AND MOODS: BEGINNER, INTERMEDIATE, AND ADVANCED LEVELS

§7.5–1 Present Indicative

This tense is used most of the time in Spanish and English. It indicates:

• An action or a state of being at the present time.

> *Hablo español.* / I speak Spanish.
> *Creo en la verdad.* / I believe in truth.

Examples:
• Habitual action.

Example:

> *Voy a la biblioteca todos los días.* / I go to the library every day.

• A general truth, something which is permanently true.

Example:

> *Seis menos dos son cuatro.* / Six minus two is four.

- Vividness when talking or writing about past events.

Example:

> *El asesino se pone pálido. Tiene miedo. Sale de la casa y corre a lo largo del río.* / The murderer turns pale. He is afraid. He goes out of the house and runs along the river.

- A near future.

Example:

> *Mi hermano llega mañana.* / My brother arrives tomorrow.

- An action or state of being that occurred in the past and continues up to the present. In Spanish this is an idiomatic use of the present tense of a verb with *hace*, which is also in the present.

Example:

> *Hace tres horas que miro la televisión.* / I have been watching television for three hours.

- The meaning of "almost" or "nearly" when used with *por poco*.

Example:

> *Por poco me matan.* / They almost killed me.

The present indicative tense is regularly formed as follows:

Drop the *ar* ending of an infinitive, like *hablar*, and add: *o, as a*; *amos, áis, an.*

You then get: *hablo, hablas, habla; hablamos, habláis, hablan.*

Drop the *er* ending of an infinitive, like *beber*, and add: *o, es, e*; *emos, éis, en.*

You then get: *bebo, bebes, bebe; bebemos, bebéis, beben.*

Drop the *ir* ending of an infinitive, like *recibir*, and add: *o, es, e*; *imos, ís, en.*

You then get: *recibo, recibes, recibe; recibimos, recibís, reciben.*

§7.5–2 Imperfect Indicative

This is a past tense. Imperfect suggests incomplete. The Imperfect tense expresses an action or a state of being that was continuous in the past and its completion is not indicated. It expresses:

• An action that was going on in the past at the same time as another action.

Example:

> *Mi hermano leía y mi padre hablaba.* / My brother was reading and my father was talking.

• An action that was going on in the past when another action occurred.

Example:

> *Mi hermana cantaba cuando yo entré.* / My sister was
> singing when I came in.

• An action that a person did habitually in the past.

Example:

> *Cuando estábamos en Nueva York, íbamos al cine todos
> los sábados.* / When we were in New York, we went to
> the movies every Saturday; When we were in New York,
> we used to go to the movies every Saturday.

• A description of a mental, emotional, or physical condition
  in the past.

Examples:

> (mental condition) *Quería ir al cine.* / I wanted to go to the
> movies.
> (emotional condition) *Estaba contento de verlo.* / I was
> happy to see him.
> (physical condition) *Mi madre era hermosa cuando era
> pequeña.* / My mother was beautiful when she was
> young.

• The time of day in the past.

Examples:

> *¿Qué hora era?* / What time was it?
> *Eran las tres.* / It was three o'clock.

• An action or state of being that occurred in the past and lasted for a certain length of time prior to another past action.

Example:

> *Hacía tres horas que miraba la televisión cuando mi hermano entró.* / I had been watching television for three hours when my brother came in.

• An indirect quotation in the past.

Example:

| Present: | *Dice que quiere venir a mi casa.* / He says he wants to come to my house. |
| Past: | *Dijo que quería venir a mi casa.* / He said he wanted to come to my house. |

The imperfect tense is regularly formed as follows:

Drop the *-ar* ending of an infinitive, like *hablar*, and add: *aba, abas, aba; ábamos, abais, aban.*

> You then get: *hablaba, hablabas, hablaba; hablábamos, hablabais, hablaban.*

The usual equivalent in English is: I was talking, I used to talk, I talked.

Drop the *-er* ending of an infinitive, like *beber*, or the *-ir* ending of an infinitive, like *recibir*, and add: *ía, ías, ía; íamos, íais, ían.*

> You then get: *bebía, bebías, bebía; bebíamos, bebíais, bebían.*

The usual equivalent in English is: I was drinking, I used to drink, I drank.

> You also get: *recibía, recibías, recibía; recibíamos, recibíais, recibían.*

The usual equivalent in English is: I was receiving, I used to receive, I received.

7.5–3 Preterit

This tense expresses an action that was completed at some time in the past.

Examples:

> *Mi padre llegó ayer.* / My father arrived yesterday.
> *María fue a la iglesia esta mañana.* / Mary went to church this morning.
> *¿Qué pasó?* / What happened?
> *Tomé el desayuno a las siete.* / I had breakfast at seven o'clock.
> *Salí de casa, tomé el autobús y llegué a la escuela a las ocho.* / I left the house, I took the bus and I arrived at school at eight o'clock.

In Spanish, some verbs have a different meaning when used in the preterit.

Examples:

Conocer	*La conocí la semana pasada en el baile.* / I met her last week at the dance.
Poder	*Pude hacerlo.* / I succeeded in doing it.
	No pude hacerlo. / I failed to do it.
Querer	*Quise llamarlo.* / I tried to call you.
	No quise hacerlo. / I refused to do it.
Saber	*Supe la verdad.* / I found out the truth.
Tener	*Tuve una carta de mi amigo Roberto.* / I received a letter from my friend Robert.

Tip	If you have studied French, don't let the Spanish preterit confuse you. In French, the passé simple (simple past) is more and more rare as it has generally been replaced by the passé composé (compound past). However, in Spanish, the preterit is used very often to express actions that were completed in the past.

The preterit tense is regularly formed as follows:

- Drop the *-ar* ending of an infinitive, like *hablar*, and add: *é, aste, ó; amos, asteis, aron.*

    You then get: *hablé, hablaste, habló, hablamos, hablasteis, hablaron.*

    The usual equivalent in English is: I talked, I did talk; you talked, you did talk, etc. I spoke, I did speak; you spoke, you did speak, etc.

- Drop the *-er* ending of an infinitive, like *beber*, or the *-ir* ending of an infinitive, like *recibir*, and add: *í, iste, ió; imos, isteis, ieron.*

    You then get: *bebí, bebiste, bebió, bebimos, bebisteis, bebieron.*

    For *recibir* you get: *recibí, recibiste, recibió; recibimos, recibisteis, recibieron.*

§7.5–4 Future

In Spanish and English, the future tense is used to express an action or a state of being that will take place at some time in the future.

> *Lo haré.* / I shall do it; I will do it.

Also, in Spanish the future tense is used to indicate:

- Conjecture regarding the present.

    > *¿Qué hora será?* / I wonder what time it is.
    > *¿Quién será?* / Who can that be? I wonder who that is.

- Probability regarding the present.

    > *Serán las cinco.* / It is probably five o'clock; It must be five o'clock.
    > *Tendrá muchos amigos.* / He probably has many friends; He must have many friends.

- An indirect quotation.

    > *María dice que vendrá mañana.* / Mary says that she will come tomorrow.

| Tip | Remember that the future is never used in Spanish after *si* when *si* means "if." |

The future tense is regularly formed as follows:

Add the following endings to the whole infinitive: *é, ás, á; emos, éis, án.*

> You then get: *hablaré, hablarás, hablará, hablaremos, hablaréis, hablarán.*

§7.5–5 Conditional

The conditional is used in Spanish and in English to express:

- An action that you would do if something else were possible.

  > *Iría a España si tuviera dinero.* / I would go to Spain if I had money.

- A conditional desire. This is a conditional of courtesy.

  > *Me gustaría tomar una limonada.* / I would like to have a lemonade.

- An indirect quotation.

  > *María dijo que vendría mañana.* / Mary said that she would come tomorrow.

  > *María decía que vendría mañana.* / Mary was saying that she would come tomorrow.

- Conjecture regarding the past.

  > *¿Quién sería?* / I wonder who that was.

- Probability regarding the past.

  > *Serían las cinco cuando salieron.* / It was probably five o'clock when they went out.

  This tense is regularly formed as follows:

  Add the following endings to the whole infinitive: *ía, ías ía; íamos, íais, ían.*

You then get: *hablaría, hablarías, hablaría, hablaríamos, hablaríais, hablarían.*

§7.5–6 Present Subjunctive

The subjunctive mood is used in Spanish much more than in English. In Spanish the present subjunctive is used:

- To express a command in the *usted* or *ustedes* form, either in the affirmative or negative.

    Siéntese Ud. / Sit down.
    No se siente Ud. / Don't sit down.

- To express a negative command in the familiar form *(tú)*.

    No te sientes. / Don't sit down.
    No duermas. / Don't sleep.

- To express a command in the first person plural, either in the affirmative or negative *(nosotros)*.

    Sentémonos. / Let's sit down.
    No entremos. / Let's not go in.

- After a verb that expresses some kind of wish, insistence, preference, suggestion, or request.

    Quiero que María lo haga. / I want Mary to do it.
    Insisto en que María lo haga. / I insist that Mary do it.

- After a verb that expresses doubt, fear, joy, hope, sorrow, or some other emotion.

    Dudo que María lo haga. / I doubt that Mary is doing it; I doubt that Mary will do it.
    No creo que María venga. / I don't believe (I doubt) that Mary is coming; I don't believe (I doubt) that Mary will come.

- After certain impersonal expressions that show necessity, doubt, regret, importance, urgency, or possibility.

    Es necesario que María lo haga. / It is necessary for Mary to do it; It is necessary that Mary do it.
    No es cierto que María venga. / It is doubtful (not certain) that Mary is coming; It is doubtful (not certain) that Mary will come.

- After certain conjunctions of time, such as *antes (de) que*, *cuando*, *en cuando*, *después (de) que*, *hasta que*, *mientras*, and the like.

  > *Le hablaré a María cuando venga.* / I shall talk to Mary when she comes.
  >
  > *Vámonos antes (de) que llueva.* / Let's go before it rains.

- After certain conjunctions that express a condition, negation, purpose, such as *a menos que*, *con tal que*, *para que*, *a fin de que*, *sin que*, *en caso (de) que*, and the like.

  > *Démelo con tal que sea bueno.* / Give it to me provided that it is good.
  >
  > *Me voy a menos que venga.* / I'm leaving unless he comes.

- After certain adverbs, such as *acaso*, *quizá*, and *tal vez*.

  > *Acaso venga mañana.* / Perhaps he will come tomorrow. Perhaps he is coming tomorrow.

- After *aunque* if the action has not yet occurred.

  > *Aunque María venga esta noche, no me quedo.* / Although Mary may come tonight, I'm not staying; Although Mary is coming tonight, I'm not staying.

- In an adjectival clause if the antecedent is something or someone that is indefinite, negative, vague, or nonexistent.

  > *Busco un libro que sea interesante.* / I'm looking for a book that is interesting.
  >
  > *¿Hay alguien aquí que hable francés?* / Is there anyone here who speaks French?
  >
  > *No hay nadie que pueda hacerlo.* / There is no one who can do it.

- After *por más que* or *por mucho que*.

  > *Por más que hable usted, no quiero escuchar.* / No matter how much you talk, I don't want to listen.

- After the expression *ojalá (que)*, which expresses a great desire or hope. This interjection means "would to God!" or "may God grant!" It is derived from Arabic.

  > *¡Ojalá que vengan mañana!* / Let's hope that they will come tomorrow!

Finally, remember that the present subjunctive is never used in Spanish after *si* when *si* means "if".

The present subjunctive of regular verbs and many irregular verbs is normally formed as follows:

Go to the present indicative, 1st person singular of the verb you have in mind, drop the ending *o*, and

- for an *-ar* ending verb, add: *e, es, e; emos, éis, en*

  You then get, for example: *hable, hables, hable; hablemos, habléis, hablen.*

- for an *-er* or *-ir* ending verb, add: *a, as a; amos, áis, an*

  You then get, for example: *beba, bebas, beba; bebamos, bebáis, beban; reciba, recibas, reciba; recibamos, recibáis, reciban.*

§7.5–7   Imperfect Subjunctive

This past tense is used for the same reasons as the *presente de subjuntivo*—that is, after certain verbs, conjunctions, impersonal expressions, etc., which were explained and illustrated above. The main difference between these two tenses is the time of the action.

If the verb in the main clause is in the present indicative (or future or present perfect indicative or imperative), the present subjunctive (or the present perfect subjunctive) is used in the dependent clause. However, you must use the present or present perfect subjunctive only when there is some element which requires the use of the subjunctive.

However, if the verb in the main clause is in the imperfect indicative, preterit, conditional, or pluperfect indicative, the imperfect subjunctive (this tense) or pluperfect subjunctive is ordinarily used in the dependent clause. However, there must be some element which requires the use of the subjunctive.

Examples:

Insistí en que María lo hiciera. / I insisted that Mary do it.

Se lo explicaba a María para que lo comprendiera. / I was explaining it to Mary so that she might understand it.

Note that the imperfect subjunctive is used after *como si* to express a condition contrary to fact.

Example:

Me habla como si fuera un niño. / He speaks to me as if I were a child.

Finally, note that *quisiera* (the imperfect subjunctive of *querer*) can be used to express in a very polite way, "I would like":

Quisiera hablar ahora. / I would like to speak now.

The imperfect subjunctive is regularly formed as follows:

For all verbs, drop the *-ron* ending of the 3rd person plural of the preterit and add the following endings:

ra, ras, ra;		se, ses, se;
ramos, rais, ran	OR	semos, seis, sen

Examples:

Preterit, 3rd Person Plural	Imperfect Subjunctive
bebieron (*beber* / to drink)	*bebiera, bebieras, bebiera; bebiéramos, bebierais, bebieran* OR *bebiese, bebieses, bebiese; bebiésemos, bebieseis, bebiesen*
dijeron (*decir* / to say, to tell)	*dijera, dijeras, dijera; dijéramos, dijerais, dijeran* OR *dijese, dijeses, dijese; dijésemos, dijeseis, dijesen*
fueron (*ir*) (*ir* / to go)	*fuera, fueras, fuera; fuéramos, fuerais, fueran* OR *fuese, fueses, fuese; fuésemos, fueseis, fuesen*

§7.5–8 Present Perfect Indicative

This tense expresses an action that took place at no definite time in the past. It is a compound tense because it is formed with the present indicative of *haber* (the auxiliary or helping verb) plus the past participle of the verb you have in mind.

> *(Yo) he hablado.* / I have spoken.
> *(Tú) no has venido a verme.* / You have not come to see me.
> *Elena ha ganado el premio.* / Helen has won the prize.

§7.5–9 Pluperfect OR Past Perfect Indicative

In Spanish and English, this past tense is used to express an action that happened in the past before another past action. Since it is used in relation to another past action, the other past action is ordinarily expressed in the preterit.

In Spanish, this tense is formed with the imperfect indicative of *haber* plus the past participle of the verb you have in mind.

> *Cuando llegué a casa, mi hermano había salido.* / When I arrived home, my brother had gone out.
> *Juan lo había perdido en la calle.* / John had lost it in the street.

§7.5–10 Past Anterior OR Preterit Perfect

This past tense is compound because it is formed with the preterit of *haber* plus the past participle of the verb you are using. It is translated into English like the pluperfect indicative explained above.

This tense is ordinarily used in formal writing, such as history and literature. It is normally used after certain conjunctions of time, e.g., *después que, cuando, apenas, luego que, en cuanto.*

Example:
Después que hubo hablado, salió. / After he had spoken, he left.

§7.5–11 Future Perfect OR Future Anterior

This compound tense is formed with the future of *haber* plus the past participle of the verb you have in mind. In Spanish and in English, this tense is used to express an action that will happen in the future before another future action. In English, this tense is formed by using "shall have" or "will have" plus the past participle of the verb you have in mind.

Example:
María llegará mañana y habré terminado mi trabajo. / Mary will arrive tomorrow, and I will have finished my work.

Also, in Spanish the future perfect is used to indicate conjecture or probability regarding recent past time.

Examples:
María se habrá acostado. / Mary has probably gone to bed; Mary must have gone to bed.
José habrá llegado. / Joseph has probably arrived; Joseph must have arrived.

§7.5–12 Conditional Perfect

This is formed with the conditional of *haber* plus the past participle of the verb you have in mind. It is used in Spanish and English to express an action that you would have done if something else had been possible; that is, you would have done something on condition that something else had been possible.

In English it is formed by using "would have" plus the past participle of the verb you have in mind.

Example:
Habría ido a España si hubiera tenido dinero. / I would have gone to Spain if I had had money.

Also, in Spanish the conditional perfect is used to indicate probability or conjecture in the past.

Examples:

Habrían sido las cinco cuando salieron. / It must have been five o'clock when they went out.

¿Quién habría sido? / Who could that have been? (or I wonder who that could have been.)

§7.5–13   Present Perfect OR Past Subjunctive

This is formed by using the present subjunctive of *haber* as the helping verb plus the past participle of the verb you have in mind.

Examples:

María duda que yo le haya hablado al profesor. / Mary doubts that I have spoken to the professor.

Siento que tú no hayas venido a verme. / I am sorry that you have not come to see me.

§7.5–14   Pluperfect OR Past Perfect Subjunctive

This is formed by using the imperfect subjunctive of *haber* as the helping verb plus the past participle of the verb you have in mind.

Examples:

Sentí mucho que no hubiera venido María. / I was very sorry that Mary had not come.

Me alegraba de que hubiera venido María. / I was glad that Mary had come.

§7.5–15   Progressive Forms of Tenses

In Spanish, there are also progressive forms of tenses. They are the progressive present and the progressive past.

- The progressive present is formed by using *estar* in the present tense plus the present participle of your main verb: *Estoy hablando.* / I am talking.
- The progressive past is formed by using *estar* in the imperfect indicative plus the present participle of your main verb: *Estaba hablando.* / I was talking.
- The progressive forms are used when you want to emphasize or intensify an action: *Estoy hablando; Estaba hablando.*

§7.5–16 Passive Voice

Passive voice means that the action of the verb falls on the subject; in other words, the subject receives the action:

> *La ventana fue abierta por el ladrón.* / The window was opened by the robber.

Note that *abierta* (really a form of the past participle *abrir / abierto*) is used as an adjective and it must agree in gender and number with the subject that it describes.

Active voice means that the subject performs the action and the subject is always stated:

> *El ladrón abrió la ventana.* / The robber opened the window.

To form the true passive, use *ser* + the past participle of the verb you have in mind; the past participle then serves as an adjective and it must agree in gender and number with the subject that it describes, as in the example given above. In the true passive, the agent (the doer) is always expressed with the preposition *por* in front of it. The formula for the true passive construction is: subject + tense of *ser* + past participle + *por* + the agent (the doer):

The reflexive pronoun *se* may be used to substitute for the

> *Estas composiciones fueron escritas por Juan.* / These compositions were written by John.

true passive voice construction. When you use the *se* construction, the subject is a thing (not a person) and the doer (agent) is not stated:

There are a few standard idiomatic expressions that are

Aquí se habla español. / Spanish is spoken here.
Aquí se hablan español e inglés. / Spanish and English are spoken here.
Se venden libros en esta tienda. / Books are sold in this store.

---

commonly used with the pronoun *se*. These expressions are not truly passive, the pronoun *se* is not truly a reflexive pronoun, and the verb form is in the 3rd person singular only. In this construction, there is no subject expressed; the subject is contained in the use of *se* + the 3rd person singular of the verb at all times and the common translations into English are: it is . . . , people . . . , they . . . , one. . . .

> *Se cree que . . .* / It is believed that . . . , people believe that . . . , they believe that . . . , one believes that . . .

Se cree que este criminal es culpable. / It is believed that this criminal is guilty.

> *Se dice que . . .* / It is said that . . . , people say that . . . , they say that . . . , one says that . . . , you say . . .

Se dice que va a nevar esta noche. / They say that it's going to snow tonight.
¿Cómo se dice en español ice cream? / How do you say "ice cream" in Spanish?

Se sabe que . . . / It is known that . . . , people know that . . . , they know that . . . , one knows that . . .

> *Se sabe que María va a casarse con Juan.* / People know that Mary is going to marry John.

The *se* reflexive pronoun construction is avoided if the subject is a person because there can be ambiguity in meaning. For example, how would you translate the following into English: *Se da un regalo.* Which of the following two meanings is intended? She (he) is being given a present, or She (he) is giving a present to himself (to herself). In correct Spanish you would have to say: *Le da (a María, a Juan,* etc.*) un regalo.* / He (she) is giving a present to Mary (to John, etc.). Avoid using the *se* construction in the passive when the subject is a person; change your sentence around and state it in the active voice to make the meaning clear. Otherwise, the pronoun *se* seems to go with the verb, as if the verb itself is reflexive, which gives an entirely different meaning. Another example: *Se miró* would mean "He (she) looked at himself (herself)," not "He (she) was looked at!" If you mean to say "He (she) looked at him (at her)," say: *La miró* or, if in the plural, say *La miraron.* / They looked at her.

§7.5–17 Imperative or Command Mood

The imperative mood is used in Spanish and in English to express a command. We saw earlier that the subjunctive mood is used to express commands in the *Ud.* and *Uds.* forms, in addition to other uses of the subjunctive mood.

Here are other points you ought to know about the imperative.

- An indirect command or deep desire expressed in the third person singular or plural is in the subjunctive. Notice the use of "Let" or "May" in the English translations. *Que* introduces this kind of command.

> *¡Que lo haga Jorge!* / Let George do it!
> *¡Que Dios se lo pague!* / May God reward you!
> *¡Que entre Roberto!* / Let Robert enter!
> *¡Que salgan!* / Let them leave!

- In some indirect commands, *que* is omitted. Here, too, the subjunctive is used.

> *¡Viva el presidente!* / Long live the president!

- The verb form of the affirmative singular familiar *(tú)* is the same as the 3rd person singular of the present indicative when expressing a command.

> *¡Entra pronto!* / Come in quickly!
> *¡Sigue leyendo!* / Keep on reading! OR Continue reading!

- There are some exceptions, however. The following verb forms are irregular in the affirmative singular imperative *(tú* form only).

di (decir)	*sal (salir)*	*val (valer)*
haz (hacer)	*sé (ser)*	*ve (ir)*
hé (haber)	*ten (tener)*	*ven (venir)*
pon (poner)		

- In the affirmative command, 1st person plural, instead of using the present subjunctive command, *vamos a* (Let's or Let us) + infinitive may be used.

> *Vamos a comer.* OR *Comamos.* / Let's eat.
> *Vamos a cantar.* OR *Cantemos.* / Let's sing.

- In the affirmative command, 1st person plural, *vamos* may be used to mean "Let's go":

> *Vamos al cine.* / Let's go to the movies.

- However, if in the negative (Let's not go), the present subjective of *ir* must be used:

> *No vayamos al cine.* / Let's not go to the movies.

- Note that *Vámonos* (1st person plural of *irse*, imperative) means "Let's go" or "Let's go away" or "Let's leave."

- Also note that *no nos vayamos* (1st person plural of *irse*, present subjunctive) means "Let's not go" or "Let's not go away" or "Let's not leave."
- The imperative in the affirmative familiar plural *(vosotros, vosotras)* is formed by dropping the final *r* of the infinitive and adding *d*.

  ¡Hablad! / Speak!   *¡Id!* / Go!
  ¡Comed! / Eat!   *¡Venid!* / Come!

- When forming the affirmative familiar plural *(vosotros, vosotras)* imperative of a reflexive verb, the final *d* on the infinitive must be dropped before the reflexive pronoun *os* is added, and both elements are joined to make one word.

  ¡Levantaos! / Get up!   *¡Sentaos!* / Sit down!

- When the final *d* is dropped in a reflexive verb ending in *-ir*, an accent mark must be written on the *i*.

  ¡Vestíos! / Get dressed!   *¡Divertíos!* / Have a good time!

- When forming the 1st person plural affirmative imperative of a reflexive verb, the final *s* must drop before the reflexive pronoun *nos* is added, and both elements are joined to make one word. This requires an accent mark on the vowel of the syllable that was stressed before *nos* was added. *Vamos + nos* changes to:

  ¡Vámonos! / Let's go! or Let's go away! or Let's leave!

- All negative imperatives in the familiar 2nd person singular *(tú)* and plural *(vosotros, vosotras)* are expressed in the present subjunctive.

  ¡No corras (tú)! / Don't run!
  ¡No corráis (vosotros or vosotras)! / Don't run!

- Object pronouns (direct, indirect, or reflexive) with an imperative verb form in the affirmative are attached to the verb form. **Examples:**

  ¡Hágalo (Ud.)! / Do it!
  ¡Díganoslo (Ud.)! / Tell it to us!
  ¡Dímelo (tú)! / Tell it to me!
  ¡Levántate (tú)! / Get up!

- Object pronouns (direct, indirect, or reflexive) with an imperative verb form in the negative are placed in front of the verb form. Compare the following examples with those given above:

> *¡No lo haga (Ud.)!* / Don't do it!
> *¡No nos lo diga (Ud.)!* / Don't tell it to us!
> *¡No me lo digas (tú)!* / Don't tell it to me!
> *¡No te levantes (tú)!* / Don't get up!

Tip

> Note that in Latin America the 2nd person plural familiar *(vosotros, vosotras)* forms are avoided. In place of them, the 3rd person plural *Uds.* forms are customarily used.

§7.5–18 Subjunctive

The subjunctive is not a tense; it is a mood or mode. Usually, when we speak in Spanish or English, we use the indicative mood. We use the subjunctive mood in Spanish for certain reasons.

After Certain Conjunctions

When the following conjunctions introduce a new clause, the verb in that new clause is in the subjunctive mood:

> *a fin de que* / so that, in order that
> *a menos que* / unless
> *como si* / as if
> *con tal que* or *con tal de que* / provided that
> *para que* / in order that, so that
> *sin que* / without

Examples:

Se lo explico a ustedes a fin de que puedan comprenderlo. / I am explaining it to you so that (in order that) you may be able to understand it.

> *Saldré a las tres y media a menos que esté lloviendo.* / I will go out at three thirty unless it is raining.

When the following conjunctions introduce a new clause, the verb in that new clause is sometimes in the indicative mood, sometimes in the subjunctive mood. Use the subjunctive mood if what is being expressed indicates some sort of anxious anticipation, doubt, indefiniteness, vagueness, or uncertainty. If these are not implied and if the action was completed in the past, use the indicative mood:

Examples:

a pesar de que / in spite of the fact that
así que / as soon as, after
aunque / although, even if, even though
cuando / when
de manera que / so that, so as
de modo que / so that, in such a way that
después que or *después de que* / after
en cuanto / as soon as
hasta que / until
luego que / as soon as, after
mientras / while, as long as
siempre que / whenever, provided that

Le daré el dinero a Roberto cuando me lo pida. / I shall (will) give the money to Robert when he asks me for it. (*Pida* is in the subjunctive mood because some doubt or uncertainty is suggested and Robert may not ask for it.)

BUT

Se lo di a Roberto cuando me lo pidió. / I gave it to Robert when he asked me for it. (No subjunctive of *pedir* here because he actually did ask me for it.)

Esperaré hasta que llegue el autobús. / I shall (will) wait until the bus arrives. (*Llegue* is in the subjunctive mood here because some doubt or uncertainty is suggested and the bus may never arrive.)

BUT

Esperé hasta que llegó el autobús. / I waited until the bus arrived. (No subjunctive of *llegar* here because the bus actually did arrive.)

After Certain Adverbs

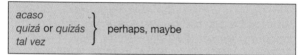

acaso
quizá or *quizás* } perhaps, maybe
tal vez

Examples:

Tal vez hayan perdido. / Perhaps they have lost. (Subjunctive is used here because some degree of uncertainty or pessimism is implied.)

Tal vez han ganado. / Perhaps they have won. (No subjunctive is used here because some degree of certainty or optimism is implied.)

> *Por* + adjective or adverb + *que* / however, no matter how

Examples:

Por (más) interesante que sea, no quiero ver esa película. / No matter how interesting it may be, I do not want to see that film.

After Certain Indefinite Expressions

cualquier, cualquiera, cualesquier, cualesquiera / whatever, whichever, any (the final *a* drops in *cualquiera* and *cualesquiera* when the word is in front of a noun)
cuandoquiera / whenever
dondequiera / wherever; *adondequiera* / to wherever
quienquiera, quienesquiera / whoever

Examples:

Dondequiera que Ud. esté, escríbame. / Wherever you may be, write to me.

Adondequiera que Ud. vaya, dígamelo. / Wherever you may go, tell me.

After an Indefinite or Negative Antecedent

The reason why the subjunctive is needed after an indefinite or negative antecedent is that the person or thing desired may possibly not exist; or, if it does exist, you may never find it.

Examples:

Busco un libro que sea interesante. (Subjunctive)
/ I am looking for a book that is interesting.

BUT

Tengo un libro que es interesante. (Indicative)
/ I have a book that is interesting.

¿Conoce Ud. a alguien que tenga paciencia? (Subjunctive)
/ Do you know someone who has patience?

BUT

Conozco a alguien que tiene paciencia. (Indicative)
/ I know someone who has patience.

No encontré a nadie que supiera la respuesta. (Subjunctive)
/ I did not find anyone who knew the answer.

BUT

Encontré a alguien que sabe la respuesta. (Indicative)
/ I found someone who knows the answer.

After ¡Que . . . !

In order to express a wish, an order, or a command indirectly in the 3rd person singular or plural, you may use the exclamatory *¡Que . . . !* alone to introduce the subjunctive clause.

¡Que lo haga Jorge! / Let George do it!
¡Que entre! / Let him enter!

After ¡Ojalá que . . . !

The exclamatory expression *Ojalá* is one of Arabic origin meaning "Oh, God!"

¡Ojalá que vengan! / If only they would come!
¡Ojalá que lleguen! / If only they would arrive!

After Certain Impersonal Expressions

> *Basta que . . .* / It is enough that . . . ; It is sufficient that . . .
> *Conviene que . . .* / It is fitting that . . . ; It is proper that . . .
> *Importa que . . .* / It is important that . . .
> *Más vale que . . .* / It is better that . . .
> *Es aconsejable que . . .* / It is advisable that . . .

Examples:
Basta que sepan la verdad. / It is sufficient that they know the truth.
Conviene que venga ahora mismo. / It is proper that she come right now.
Es aconsejable que salga inmediatamente. / It is advisable that she leave immediately.

After Verbs or Expressions That Indicate Denial, Doubt or Lack of Belief, and Uncertainty

> *dudar que . . .* / to doubt that . . .
> *negar que . . .* / to deny that . . .
> *no creer que . . .* / not to believe that . . .
> *Es dudoso que . . .* / It is doubtful that . . .
> *Es incierto que . . .* / It is uncertain that . . .
> *Hay duda que . . .* / There is doubt that . . .
> *No es cierto que . . .* / It is not certain that . . .
> *No estar seguro que . . .* / Not to be sure that . . .

Dudo que mis amigos vengan. / I doubt that my friends are coming.
No creo que sea urgente. / I do not believe that it is urgent.

Tip

You may still have doubts about when to use the subjunctive mood. Remember that doubt requires the use of the subjunctive:

Es dudoso que vayas a aprender el subjuntivo sin estudiar. / It is doubtful that you are going to learn the subjunctive without studying.

After Verbs or Expressions That Indicate an Emotion

estar contento de que . . . / to be happy that . . . , to be
pleased that . . .
estar feliz que . . . / to be happy that . . .
estar triste que . . . / to be sad that . . .
alegrarse (de) que . . . / to be glad that . . .
sentir que . . . / to regret that . . . , to feel sorry that . . .

Examples:
Estoy muy contento de que mis amigos vengan a verme. / I am
very pleased that my friends are coming (will come) to see me.
Me alegro de que ellos hayan venido. / I am glad that they have
come.

After Certain Verbs That Imply a Wish or Desire That Something Be Done, Including a Command, Order, Preference, Advice, Permission, Request, Plea, Insistence, or Suggestion

aconsejar / to advise
decir / to tell (someone to do something)
desear / to want, to wish
mandar / to order, to command
pedir / to ask, to request
preferir / to prefer
prohibir / to forbid, to prohibit
querer / to want, to wish
rogar / to beg, to request
sugerir / to suggest

Examples:

Les aconsejo a ellos que hagan el trabajo. / I advise them to do the work.

Les digo a ellos que escriban los ejercicios. / I am telling them to write the exercises.

Mi madre quiere que yo vaya a la escuela. / My mother wants me to go to school.

BUT

Yo quiero ir a la escuela. / I want to go to school.

Note: In this example, there is no change in subject; therefore, the infinitive *ir* is used. But in the example above, beginning with *Mi madre quiere que . . .*, there is a new subject *(yo)* in the dependent clause and *ir* is in the subjunctive because the verb *querer* is used in the main clause.

El capitán me manda que yo entre. / The captain orders me to come in.

Sequence of Tenses When The Subjunctive Is Required: A Summary

When the verb in the main clause is in the: ↓	The verb in the following clause (the dependent clause) most likely will be in the: ↓
Present indicative or Future or Present perfect indicative or Imperative (Command)	Present subjunctive or Present perfect subjunctive
Conditional or a past tense (Imperfect indicative or Preterit or Pluperfect indicative)	Imperfect subjunctive or Pluperfect subjunctive

Examples:

Deseo que Ana cante. / I want Anna to sing.

Le diré a Ana que baile. / I will tell Anna to dance.

Le he dicho a Ana que cante y baile. / I have said to Anna to sing and dance.

Dígale a Ana que cante y baile. / Tell Anna to sing and dance.

Dudo que mi madre tome el tren. / I doubt that my mother is taking the train.

§7.5–19 The Names of Tenses and Moods

The Simple Tenses	The Compound Tenses
Present indicative	Present perfect indicative
Imperfect indicative	Pluperfect OR Past perfect indicative
Preterit	Past anterior OR Preterit perfect
Future	Future perfect OR Future anterior
Conditional	Conditional perfect
Present subjunctive	Present perfect OR Past subjunctive
Imperfect subjunctive	Pluperfect OR Past perfect subjunctive
Imperative OR Command	

Note: The subject pronouns in Spanish are omitted below in order to emphasize the verb forms.

Singular:	*yo, tú, Ud.* OR *él* OR *ella*;
Plural:	*nosotros (nosotras), vosotros (vosotras), Uds.* OR *ellos* OR *ellas*

Haber (helping verb) in the 7 simple tenses

Present participle: *habiendo*
Past participle: *habido*
Infinitive: *haber*

Present indicative	*he, has, ha; hemos, habéis, han* I have, you have, you or he or she or it has; we have, you have, you or they have
Imperfect indicative	*había, habías, había; habíamos, habíais, habían* I had, you had, you or he or she or it had; we had, you had, you or they had
Preterit	*hube, hubiste, hubo; hubimos, hubisteis, hubieron* I had, you had, you or he or she or it had; we had, you had, you or they had
Future	*habré, habrás, habrá; habremos, habréis, habrán* I shall (will) have, you will have, you or he or she or it will have; we shall (will) have, you will have, you or they will have
Conditional	*habría, habrías, habría; habríamos, habríais, habrían* I would have, you would have, you or he or she or it would have; we would have, you would have, you or they would have

Present subjunctive	*haya*, *hayas*, *haya*; *hayamos*, *hayáis*, *hayan*
	that I may have, that you may have, that you or he or she or it may have; that we may have, that you may have, that you or they may have
Imperfect subjunctive	(the *-ra* form): *hubiera*, *hubieras*, *hubiera*; *hubiéramos*, *hubierais*, *hubieran*
	OR
	(the *-se* form): *hubiese*, *hubieses*, *hubiese*; *hubiésemos*, *hubieseis*, *hubiesen*
	that I might have, that you might have, that you or he or she or it might have; that we might have, that you might have, that you or they might have

§7.6 SPECIAL CASES AND VERBS WITH SPECIAL MEANINGS

§7.6–1 *Si* Clause: A Summary of Contrary-to-Fact Conditions

When the verb in the *Si* clause is:	The verb in the main or result clause is:
Present indicative	Future

Example:

Si tengo bastante tiempo, vendré a verle. / If I have enough time, I will come to see you.

When the verb in the *Si* clause is:	The verb in the main or result clause is:

Note that the present subjunctive form of a verb is never used in a clause beginning with the conjunction *si*.

Imperfect subjunctive (-*se* form or -*ra* form)	Conditional or Imperfect subjunctive (-*ra* form)

Example:

Si yo tuviese (or *tuviera*) *bastante tiempo, vendría a verle.* / If I had enough time, I would come to see you.

OR

Si yo tuviese (or *tuviera*) *bastante tiempo, viniera a verle.* / If I had enough time, I would come to see you.

Pluperfect subjunctive (-*se* form or -*ra* form)	Conditional perfect or Pluperfect subjunctive (-*ra* form)

Example:

Si yo hubiese tenido (or *hubiera tenido*) *bastante tiempo, habría venido a verle.* / If I had had enough time, I would have come to see you.

OR

Si yo hubiese tenido (or *hubiera tenido*) *bastante tiempo, hubiera venido a verle.* / If I had had enough time, I would have come to see you.

§7.6–2 *Acabar de* + Infinitive

In the present indicative:

María acaba de llegar. / Mary has just arrived.
Acabo de comer. / I have just eaten.
Acabamos de terminar la lección. / We have just finished the lesson.

When you use *acabar* in the present tense, it indicates that the action of the main verb (+ infinitive) has just occurred now in the present. In English, we express this by using have just + the past participle of the main verb.

In the imperfect indicative:

> *María acababa de llegar.* / Mary had just arrived.
> *(Yo) acababa de comer.* / I had just eaten.
> *Acabábamos de terminar la lección.* / We had just finished the lesson.

When you use *acabar* in the imperfect indicative, it indicates that the action of the main verb (+ infinitive) had occurred at some time in the past when another action occurred. In English, we express this by using had just + the past participle of the main verb.

§7.6–3 *Conocer* and *saber*

These two verbs mean "to know," but they are used differently.

- *Conocer* means "to know" in the sense of being acquainted with a person, a place, or a thing:

> *¿Conoce Ud. a María?* / Do you know Mary?
> *¿Conoce Ud. bien los Estados Unidos?* / Do you know the United States well?
> *¿Conoce Ud. este libro?* / Do you know (Are you acquainted with) this book?

In the preterit tense, *conocer* means "met" in the sense of first met, first became acquainted with someone:

> *¿Conoce Ud. a Elena?* / Do you know Helen?
> *Sí, (yo) la conocí anoche en casa de un amigo mío.* / Yes, I met her [for the first time] last night at the home of one of my friends.

- *Saber* means to know a fact, to know something thoroughly:

> *¿Sabe Ud. qué hora es?* / Do you know what time it is?

When you use *saber* + infinitive, it means to know how:

> *¿Sabe Ud. nadar?* / Do you know how to swim?
> *Sí, (yo) sé nadar.* / Yes, I know how to swim.

In the preterit tense, *saber* means "found out":

> *¿Lo sabe Ud.?* / Do you know it?
> *Sí, lo supe ayer.* / Yes, I found it out yesterday.

§7.6–4   *Deber, deber de,* and *tener que*

Generally speaking, use *deber* when you want to express a moral obligation, something you ought to do but you may or may not do:

> *Debo estudiar esta noche pero estoy cansado y no me siento bien.* / I ought to study tonight, but I am tired, and I do not feel well.

Generally speaking, *deber de* + infinitive is used to express a supposition, something that is probable:

> *La señora Gómez debe de estar enferma porque sale de casa raramente.* / Mrs. Gómez must be sick (is probably sick) because she rarely goes out of the house.

Generally speaking, use *tener que* when you want to say that you have to do something:

> *No puedo salir esta noche porque tengo que estudiar.* / I cannot go out tonight because I have to study.

§7.6–5   *Dejar, salir,* and *salir de*

These verbs mean to leave, but notice the uses:

Use *dejar* when you leave someone or when you leave something behind you:

> *El alumno dejó sus libros en la sala de clase.* / The pupil left his books in the classroom.

Dejar also means to let or to allow or to let go:

> *¡Déjelo!* / Let it! (Leave it!)

Use *salir de* when you mean to leave in the sense of to go out of (a place):

El alumno salió de la sala de clase. / The pupil left the classroom.
¿Dónde está su madre? Mi madre salió. / Where is your mother?
My mother went out.

§7.6–6 *Dejar de* + Infinitive and *dejar caer*

Use *dejar de* + infinitive when you mean to stop or to fail to:

Los alumnos dejaron de hablar. / The students stopped talking.
¡No deje Ud. de llamarme! / Don't fail to call me!

Dejar caer means to drop:

Luis dejó caer sus libros. / Louis dropped his books.

§7.6–7 *Ir, irse*

Use *ir* when you simply mean "to go":

Voy al cine. / I am going to the movies.

Use *irse* when you mean "to leave" in the sense of "to go away":

Mis padres se fueron al campo para visitar a mis abuelos. / My
parents left for (went away to) the country to visit my
grandparents.

§7.6–8 *Gastar* and *pasar*

These two verbs mean "to spend," but notice the uses:

Use *gastar* when you spend money:

No me gusta gastar mucho dinero. / I don't like to spend much
money.

Use *pasar* when you spend time:

Me gustaría pasar un año en España. / I would like to spend a
year in Spain.

§7.6–9 *Gustar*

Essentially, the verb *gustar* means "to be pleasing to . . ."
- In English, we say, for example, I like ice cream. In Spanish,
we say *Me gusta el helado.*
- In English, the thing that you like is the direct object. In
Spanish, the thing that you like is the subject. Also, in
Spanish, the person who likes the thing is the indirect
object: to me, to you, etc.:

A Roberto le gusta el helado. / Robert likes ice cream; in other words, "To Robert, ice cream is pleasing (to him/*le*)."

- In Spanish, therefore, the verb *gustar* is used in the third person, either in the singular or plural, when you talk about something that you like—something that is pleasing to you. Therefore, the verb form must agree with the subject; if the thing that is liked is singular, the verb is third person singular; if the thing that is liked is plural, the verb *gustar* is third person plural:

  Me gusta el café. / I like coffee.
  Me gustan el café y la leche. / I like coffee and milk.

- When you mention the person or the persons who like something, you must use the preposition *a* in front of the person:

  A los muchachos y a las muchachas les gusta jugar. / Boys and girls like to play; that is to say, "To play is pleasing to them, to boys and girls."

  Did you notice the indirect object pronoun *les* in *les gusta jugar?* You must also use the indirect object pronoun of the noun that is the person or persons (*los muchachos* and *las muchachas*).

- Review the indirect object pronouns, which are *me, te, le; nos, os, les.*

Tip	
	Me gusta leer. / I like to read.
	Te gusta leer. / You (fam.) like to read.
	A Felipe le gustan el helado. / Philip likes ice cream.
	Al chico le gustan los videojuegos. / The boy likes video games.
	A Carlota le gusta bailar. / Charlotte likes to dance.
	A las chicas les gustó la película. / The girls liked the movie.
	Nos gustó el cuento. / We liked the story.

§7.6–10   *Haber, haber de* + Infinitive, and *tener*

The verb *haber* (to have) is used as an auxiliary verb (or helping verb) in order to form the seven compound tenses.

The verb *haber* is also used to form the perfect (or past) infinitive: *haber hablado* (to have spoken). This is formed by using the infinitive form of *haber* + the past participle of the main verb. (See §7.3–1.)

The verb *haber* is also used to form the perfect participle: *habiendo hablado* (having spoken). This is formed by using the present participle of *haber* + the past participle of the main verb.

The verb *haber* + *de* + infinitive is equivalent to the English use of "to be supposed to . . . ."

Example:
María ha de traer un pastel y yo he de traer el helado. / Mary is supposed to bring a pie and I am supposed to bring the ice cream.

The verb *tener* is used to mean "to have" in the sense of "to possess" or "to hold":

Tengo un perro y un gato. / I have a dog and a cat.

In the preterit tense, *tener* can mean "received":

Ayer mi padre tuvo un cheque. / Yesterday my father received a check.

§7.6–11   *Jugar* and *tocar*

Both these verbs mean "to play", but they have different uses. *Jugar a* means "to play a sport, a game":

¿Juega Ud. al tenis? / Do you play tennis?
Me gusta jugar a la pelota. / I like to play ball.

The verb *tocar* means to play a musical instrument:

Carmen toca muy bien el piano. / Carmen plays the piano very well.

The verb *tocar* has other meanings: "to be one's turn," in which case it takes an indirect object:

> *¿A quién le toca?* / Whose turn is it?
> *Le toca a Juan.* / It is John's turn.

To knock on a door:

> *tocar a la puerta; Alguien toca a la puerta.* / Someone is knocking on (at) the door.

Essentially, *tocar* means "to touch."

§7.6–12 *Llegar a ser, hacerse,* and *ponerse*

These three verbs mean "to become." Note the uses:

Use *llegar a ser* + a noun: to become a doctor, to become a teacher; in other words, the noun indicates the goal that you are striving for:

> *Quiero llegar a ser doctor.* / I want to become a doctor.

Hacerse is used similarly:

> *Juan se hizo abogado.* / John became a lawyer.

Use *ponerse* + an adjective: to become pale, to become sick; in other words, the adjective indicates the state or condition (physical or mental) that you have become:

> *Cuando vi el accidente, me puse pálido.* / When I saw the accident, I became pale.
> *Mi madre se puso triste al oír la noticia desgraciada.* / My mother became sad upon hearing the unfortunate news.

§7.6–13 *Llevar* and *tomar*

These two verbs mean "to take." However, they are used differently:

Llevar means "to take" in the sense of "to carry" or "to transport from place to place":

> *José llevó la silla de la cocina al comedor.* / Joseph took the chair from the kitchen to the dining room.

The verb *llevar* is also used when you take someone somewhere:

Pedro llevó a María al baile anoche. / Peter took Mary to the dance last night.

As you probably know, *llevar* also means to "wear":

María, ¿por qué llevas la falda nueva? / Mary, why are you wearing your new skirt?

Tomar means "to take" in the sense of "grab" or "catch":

La profesora tomó el libro y comenzó a leer a la clase. / The teacher took the book and began to read to the class.
Mi amigo tomó el tren esta mañana a las siete. / My friend took the train this morning at seven o'clock.

§7.6–14 *Pedir* and *preguntar*

Both these verbs mean "to ask" but note the uses:
   Pedir means "to ask for something" or "to request":

El alumno pidió un lápiz al profesor. / The pupil asked the teacher for a pencil.

Preguntar means to inquire or "to ask a question":

La alumna preguntó a la profesora cómo estaba. / The pupil asked the teacher how she was.

§7.6–15 *Pensar de* and *pensar en*

Both these verbs mean "to think of," but note the uses:
   Pensar is used with the preposition *de* when you ask someone what he/she thinks of someone or something, when you ask for someone's opinion:

¿Qué piensa Ud. de este libro? / What do you think of this book?
Pienso que es bueno. / I think that it is good.

Pensar is used with the preposition *en* when you ask someone what or whom he/she is thinking about:

Miguel, no hablas mucho; ¿en qué piensas? / Michael, you are not talking much; of what are you thinking? (what are you thinking of?)
Pienso en las vacaciones de verano. / I'm thinking of summer vacation.

§7.6–16 *Poder* and *saber*

Both these verbs mean "can" but note the uses:

Poder means "can" in the sense of ability:

> *No puedo ayudarle; lo siento.* / I cannot (am unable to) help you;
> I'm sorry.

Saber means "can" in the sense of "to know how":

> *Este niño no sabe contar.* / This child can't (does not know how
> to) count.

In the preterit tense, *poder* has the special meaning of "succeeded":

> *Después de algunos minutos, Juan pudo abrir la puerta.* / After a
> few minutes, John succeeded in opening the door.

In the preterit tense, *saber* has the special meaning of "found out":

> *Lo supe ayer.* / I found it out yesterday.

§7.6–17 *Ser* and *estar*

These two verbs mean "to be" but note the uses:

Generally speaking, use *ser* when you want to express "to be."

Use *estar* when "to be" is used in the following ways:

Health:

> *¿Cómo está Ud.?* / How are you?
> *Estoy bien.* / I am well.
> *Estoy enfermo (enferma).* / I am sick.

Location: persons, places, things

> *Estoy en la sala de clase.* / I am in the classroom.
> *La escuela está lejos.* / The school is far.
> *Barcelona está en España.* / Barcelona is (located) in Spain.

State or condition: persons

> *Estoy contento (contenta).* / I am happy.
> *Los alumnos están cansados. (Las alumnas están cansadas.)* /
> The students are tired.

María está triste hoy. / Mary is sad today.
Estoy listo (lista). / I am ready.
Estoy pálido (pálida). / I am pale.
Estoy ocupado (ocupada). / I am busy.

State or condition: things and places

La ventana está abierta. / The window is open.
La taza está llena. / The cup is full.
El té está caliente. / The tea is hot.

To form the progressive present of a verb, use the present tense of *estar* + the present participle of the main verb.

Estoy estudiando en mi cuarto y no puedo salir esta noche. / I am studying in my room, and I cannot go out tonight.

To form the progressive past of a verb, use the imperfect tense of *estar* + the present participle of the main verb.

Mi hermano estaba leyendo cuando (yo) entré en el cuarto. / My brother was reading when I entered (came into) the room.

§7.6–18 *Volver* and *devolver*

These two verbs mean "to return" but note the uses:
Volver means "to return" in the sense of "come back":

Voy a volver a casa. / I am going to return home.

A synonym of *volver* is *regresar*:

Los muchachos regresaron a las ocho de la noche. / The boys came back at eight o'clock in the evening.

Devolver means "to return" in the sense of "give back":

Voy a devolver el libro a la biblioteca. / I am going to return the book to the library.

§7.7 COMMONLY USED IRREGULAR VERBS

In Various Tenses, Including Stem-Changing Verbs and Orthographically Changing Verbs (Verbs That Change In Spelling)

§7.7–1 Present Indicative

acordarse / to remember
me acuerdo,
te acuerdas, se acuerda;
nos acordamos,
os acordáis, se acuerdan

acostarse / to go to bed, to lie down
me acuesto, te acuestas,
se acuesta;
nos acostamos,
os acostáis, se acuestan

almorzar / to lunch, to have lunch
almuerzo, almuerzas,
almuerza; almorzamos,
almorzáis, almuerzan

aparecer / to appear, to show up
aparezco, apareces,
aparece; aparecemos,
aparecéis, aparecen

caber / to fit, to be contained
quepo, cabes, cabe;
cabemos, cabéis, caben

caer / to fall
caigo, caes, cae;
caemos, caéis, caen

cerrar / to close
cierro, cierras, cierra;
cerramos, cerráis, cierran

cocer / to cook
cuezo, cueces, cuece;
cocemos, cocéis, cuecen

coger / to seize, to grasp, to grab, to catch
cojo, coges, coge;
cogemos, cogéis, cogen

comenzar / to begin, to start, to commence
comienzo, comienzas,
comienza; comenzamos,
comenzáis, comienzan

conducir / to conduct, to lead, to drive
conduzco, conduces,
conduce; conducimos,
conducís, conducen

conocer / to know, to be acquainted with
conozco, conoces,
conoce; conocemos,
conocéis, conocen

contar / to count, to relate
cuento, cuentas, cuenta;
contamos, contáis,
cuentan

corregir / to correct
corrijo, corriges, corrige;
corregimos, corregís,
corrigen

costar / to cost
cuesta; cuestan

dar / to give
doy, das, da; damos,
dais, dan

decir / to say, to tell
digo, dices, dice;
decimos, decís, dicen

despertarse / to awaken, to wake up (oneself)
me despierto,

te despiertas,
se despierta;
nos despertamos,
os despertáis,
se despiertan

devolver / to return, to give back
(something)
devuelvo, devuelves,
devuelve; devolvemos,
devolvéis, devuelven

divertirse / to have a good time, to
enjoy oneself
me divierto, te diviertes,
se divierte;
nos divertimos,
os divertís, se divierten

doler / to ache, to pain, to hurt, to
cause grief, to cause regret
duelo, dueles, duele;
dolemos, doléis, duelen

dormir / to sleep
duermo, duermes,
duerme; dormimos,
dormís, duermen

dormirse / to fall asleep
me duermo, te duermes,
se duerme;
nos dormimos,
os dormís, se duermen

empezar / to begin, to start
empiezo, empiezas,
empieza, empezamos,
empezáis, empiezan

encontrar / to meet, to encounter, to
find
encuentro, encuentras,
encuentra; encontramos,
encontráis, encuentran

entender / to understand
entiendo, entiendes,
entiende; entendemos,
entendéis, entienden

enviar / to send
envío, envías, envía;
enviamos, enviáis, envían

estar / to be
estoy, estás, está;
estamos, estáis, están

haber / to have (as an auxiliary or
helping verb)
he, has, ha; hemos,
habéis, han

hacer / to do, to make
hago, haces, hace;
hacemos, hacéis, hacen

helar / to freeze
hiela OR está helando (in the
present progressive form)

ir / to go
voy, vas, va; vamos,
vais, van

irse / to go away
me voy, te vas, se va;
nos vamos, os vais,
se van

jugar / to play
juego, juegas, juega;
jugamos, jugáis, juegan

llover / to rain
llueve OR está lloviendo
(in the present progressive form)

morir / to die
muero, mueres, muere;
morimos, morís, mueren

mostrar / to show, to point out
muestro, muestras,
muestra; mostramos,
mostráis, muestran

nacer / to be born
nazco, naces, nace;
nacemos, nacéis, nacen

nevar / to snow
nieva OR está nevando
(in the present progressive form)

obtener / to obtain, to get
obtengo, obtienes,
obtiene; obtenemos,
obtenéis, obtienen

oír / to hear
oigo, oyes, oye; oímos,
oís, oyen

pedir / to ask for, to request
pido, pides, pide;
pedimos, pedís, piden

pensar / to think
pienso, piensas, piensa;
pensamos, pensáis,
piensan

perder / to lose
pierdo, pierdes, pierde;
perdemos, perdéis,
pierden

poder / to be able, can
puedo, puedes, puede;
podemos, podéis, pueden

poner / to put, to place
pongo, pones, pone;
ponemos, ponéis, ponen

querer / to want, to wish
quiero, quieres, quiere;
queremos, queréis,
quieren

recordar / to remember
recuerdo, recuerdas,
recuerda; recordamos,
recordáis, recuerdan

reír / to laugh
río, ríes, ríe; reímos, reís,
ríen

repetir / to repeat
repito, repites, repite;
repetimos, repetís,
repiten

saber / to know, to know how
sé, sabes, sabe;
sabemos, sabéis, saben

salir / to go out
salgo, sales, sale;
salimos, salís, salen

seguir / to follow, to pursue, to
continue
sigo, sigues, sigue;
seguimos, seguís, siguen

sentarse / to sit down
me siento, te sientas,
se sienta; nos sentamos,
os sentáis, se sientan

sentir / to feel sorry, to regret, to
feel, to experience, to sense
siento, sientes, siente;
sentimos, sentís, sienten

sentirse / to feel (well, sick)
me siento, te sientes,

se siente; nos sentimos,
os sentís, se sienten

ser / to be
soy, eres, es; somos,
sois, son

servir / to serve
sirvo, sirves, sirve;
servimos, servís, sirven

soñar / to dream
sueño, sueñas, sueña;
soñamos, soñáis, sueñan

sonreír / to smile
sonrío, sonríes, sonríe;
sonreímos, sonreís,
sonríen

tener / to have, to hold
tengo, tienes, tiene;
tenemos, tenéis, tienen

traer / to bring
traigo, traes, trae;
traemos, traéis, traen

venir / to come
vengo, vienes, viene;
venimos, venís, vienen

ver / to see
veo, ves, ve; vemos, veis, ven

volver / to return
vuelvo, vuelves, vuelve;
volvemos, volvéis, vuelven

§7.7–2 Imperfect Indicative

ir / to go (I was going, I used to go,
etc.)
iba, ibas, iba; íbamos,
ibais, iban

ser / to be (I was, I used to be, etc.)
era, eras, era; éramos,
erais, eran

ver / to see (I was seeing, I used to
see, etc.)
veía, veías, veía;
veíamos, veíais, veían

§7.7–3 Preterit (Irregular Forms, Including Stem-Changing and Orthographically Changing)

acercarse / to approach, to draw
near
me acerqué,
te acercaste, se acercó;
nos acercamos,
os acercasteis,

se acercaron

almorzar / to have lunch, to eat
lunch
almorcé, almorzaste,
almorzó; almorzamos,
almorzasteis, almorzaron

andar / to walk
anduve, anduviste, anduvo; anduvimos, anduvisteis, anduvieron

buscar / to look for, to search, to seek
busqué, buscaste, buscó; buscamos, buscasteis, buscaron

caber / to fit, to be contained
cupe, cupiste, cupo; cupimos, cupisteis, cupieron

caer / to fall
caí, caíste, cayó; caímos, caísteis, cayeron

comenzar / to begin, to commence, to start
comencé, comenzaste, comenzó; comenzamos, comenzasteis, comenzaron

conducir / to conduct, to lead, to drive
conduje, condujiste, condujo; condujimos, condujisteis, condujeron

creer / to believe
creí, creíste, creyó; creímos, creísteis, creyeron

dar / to give
di, diste, dio; dimos, disteis, dieron

decir / to say, to tell
dije, dijiste, dijo; dijimos, dijisteis, dijeron

detener / to detain, to stop (someone or something)
detuve, detuviste, detuvo; detuvimos, detuvisteis, detuvieron

detenerse / to stop (oneself or itself)
me detuve, te detuviste, se detuvo; nos detuvimos, os detuvisteis, se detuvieron

estar / to be
estuve, estuviste, estuvo; estuvimos, estuvisteis, estuvieron

haber / to have (as an auxiliary or helping verb)
hube, hubiste, hubo; hubimos, hubisteis, hubieron

hacer / to do, to make
hice, hiciste, hizo; hicimos, hicisteis, hicieron

ir / to go
fui, fuiste, fue; fuimos, fuisteis, fueron

irse / to go away
me fui, te fuiste, se fue; nos fuimos, os fuisteis, se fueron

leer / to read
leí, leíste, leyó; leímos, leísteis, leyeron

llegar / to arrive
llegué, llegaste, llegó; llegamos, llegasteis, llegaron

oír / to hear (sometimes can mean

"to understand")
oí, oíste, oyó; oímos,
oísteis, oyeron

poder / to be able, can
pude, pudiste, pudo;
pudimos, pudisteis, pudieron

poner / to put, to place
puse, pusiste, puso;
pusimos, pusisteis,
pusieron

querer / to want, to wish
quise, quisiste, quiso;
quisimos, quisisteis,
quisieron

reír / to laugh
reí, reíste, rió; reímos,
reísteis, rieron

saber / to know, to know how
supe, supiste, supo;
supimos, supisteis,
supieron

ser / to be
fui, fuiste, fue; fuimos,
fuisteis, fueron
Note that these forms are the
same for *ir* in the preterit.

tener / to have, to hold
tuve, tuviste, tuvo;
tuvimos, tuvisteis,
tuvieron

traer / to bring
traje, trajiste, trajo;
trajimos, trajisteis,
trajeron

venir / to come
vine, viniste, vino;
vinimos, vinisteis, vinieron

ver / to see
vi, viste, vio; vimos,
visteis, vieron

§7.7–4 Future (Irregular Forms, Including Stem-Changing and Orthographically Changing)

caber / to fit, to be contained
cabré, cabrás, cabrá;
cabremos, cabréis,
cabrán

decir / to say, to tell
diré, dirás, dirá; diremos,
diréis, dirán

haber / to have (as an auxiliary or
helping verb)
habré, habrás, habrá;
habremos, habréis,
habrán

hacer / to do, to make
haré, harás, hará;
haremos, haréis, harán

poder / to be able, can
podré, podrás, podrá;
podremos, podréis,
podrán

poner / to put, to place
pondré, pondrás,
pondrá; pondremos,
pondréis, pondrán

querer / to want, to wish
 querré, querrás, querrá;
 querremos, querréis,
 querrán

saber / to know, to know how
 sabré, sabrás, sabrá;
 sabremos, sabréis,
 sabrán

salir / to go out
 saldré, saldrás, saldrá;
 saldremos, saldréis,
 saldrán

tener / to have, to hold
 tendré, tendrás, tendrá;
 tendremos, tendréis,
 tendrán

valer / to be worth, to be worthy
 valdré, valdrás, valdrá;
 valdremos, valdréis,
 valdrán

venir / to come
 vendré, vendrás, vendrá;
 vendremos, vendréis,
 vendrán

§7.7–5 Conditional

caber / to fit, to be contained
 cabría, cabrías, cabría;
 cabríamos, cabríais,
 cabrían

decir / to say, to tell
 diría, dirías, diría;
 diríamos, diríais, dirían

haber / to have (as an auxiliary or
 helping verb)
 habría, habrías, habría;
 habríamos, habríais,
 habrían

hacer / to do, to make
 haría, harías, haría;
 haríamos, haríais, harían

poder / to be able, can
 podría, podrías, podría;
 podríamos, podríais,
 podrían

poner / to put, to place
 pondría, pondrías,

pondría; pondríamos,
 pondríais, pondrían

querer / to want, to wish
 querría querrías, querría;
 querríamos, querríais,
 querrían

saber / to know, to know how
 sabría, sabrías, sabría;
 sabríamos, sabríais,
 sabrían

salir / to go out
 saldría, saldrías, saldría;
 saldríamos, saldríais,
 saldrían

tener / to have, to hold
 tendría, tendrías, tendría;
 tendríamos, tendríais,
 tendrían

valer / to be worth, to be worthy
 valdría, valdrías, valdría;
 valdríamos, valdríais,
 valdrían

venir / to come
vendría, vendrías,

vendría; vendríamos,
vendríais, vendrían

§7.7–6 Present Subjunctive

dar / to give
dé, des, dé; demos, deis,
den

estar / to be
esté, estés, esté;
estemos, estéis, estén

haber / to have (as an auxiliary or
helping verb)
haya, hayas, haya;
hayamos, hayáis, hayan

ir / to go
vaya, vayas, vaya;
vayamos, vayáis, vayan

saber / to know, to know how
sepa, sepas, sepa;
sepamos, sepáis, sepan

ser / to be
sea, seas, sea; seamos,
seáis, sean

§7.7–7 Imperfect Subjunctive

beber / to drink
bebiera, bebieras,
bebiera; bebiéramos,
bebierais, bebieran

OR

bebiese, bebieses,
bebiese; bebiésemos,
bebieseis, bebiesen

dar / to give
diera, dieras, diera;
diéramos, dierais, dieran

OR

diese, dieses, diese;
diésemos, dieseis, diesen

hablar / to speak
hablara, hablaras,
hablara; habláramos,
hablarais, hablaran

OR

hablase, hablases,
hablase; hablásemos,
hablaseis, hablasen

leer / to read
leyera, leyeras, leyera;
leyéramos, leyerais, leyeran

OR

leyese, leyeses, leyese;
leyésemos, leyeseis, leyesen

recibir / to receive
  recibiera, recibieras,
  recibiera; recibiéramos,
  recibierais, recibieran
          OR
  recibiese, recibieses,
  recibiese; recibiésemos,
  recibieseis, recibiesen

tener / to have
  tuviera, tuvieras, tuviera;
  tuviéramos, tuvierais,
  tuvieran
          OR
  tuviese, tuvieses,
  tuviese; tuviésemos,
  tuvieseis, tuviesen

§7.7–8 Complete Conjugations

Here are four commonly used irregular verbs conjugated fully
in all the tenses and moods.

In the format of the verbs that follow, the subject pronouns
have been omitted in order to emphasize the verb forms. The
subject pronouns are:

Singular	Plural
yo	*nosotros (nosotras)*
tú	*vosotros (vosotras)*
Ud. (él, ella)	*Uds. (ellos, ellas)*

estar / to be

(gerundio)
Present Participle: *estando*   Past Participle: *estado*

Singular	**Plural**	**Singular**	**Plural**
Present Indicative		Present Perfect Indicative	
estoy	*estamos*	*he estado*	*hemos estado*
estás	*estáis*	*has estado*	*habéis estado*
está	*están*	*ha estado*	*han estado*
Imperfect Indicative		Pluperfect OR Past Perfect Indicative	
estaba	*estábamos*	*había estado*	*habíamos estado*
estabas	*estabais*	*habías estado*	*habíais estado*
estaba	*estaban*	*había estado*	*habían estado*
Preterit		Past Anterior OR Preterit Perfect	
estuve	*estuvimos*	*hube estado*	*hubimos estado*
estuviste	*estuvisteis*	*hubiste estado*	*hubisteis estado*
estuvo	*estuvieron*	*hubo estado*	*hubieron estado*
Future		Future Perfect OR Future Anterior	
estaré	*estaremos*	*habré estado*	*habremos estado*
estarás	*estaréis*	*habrás estado*	*habréis estado*
estará	*estarán*	*habrá estado*	*habrán estado*
Conditional		Conditional Perfect	
estaría	*estaríamos*	*habría estado*	*habríamos estado*
estarías	*estaríais*	*habrías estado*	*habríais estado*
estaría	*estarían*	*habría estado*	*habrían estado*
Present Subjunctive		Present Perfect OR Past Subjunctive	
esté	*estemos*	*haya estado*	*hayamos estado*
estés	*estéis*	*hayas estado*	*hayáis estado*
esté	*estén*	*haya estado*	*hayan estado*
Imperfect Subjunctive		Pluperfect OR Past Perfect Subjunctive	
estuviera	*estuviéramos*	*hubiera estado*	*hubiéramos estado*
estuvieras	*estuvierais*	*hubieras estado*	*hubierais estado*
estuviera	*estuvieran*	*hubiera estado*	*hubieran estado*
OR		OR	
estuviese	*estuviésemos*	*hubiese estado*	*hubiésemos estado*
estuvieses	*estuvieseis*	*hubieses estado*	*hubieseis estado*
estuviese	*estuviesen*	*hubiese estado*	*hubiesen estado*

Imperative	
—	*estemos*
está; no estés	*estad; no estéis*
esté	*estén*

hacer / to do, to make

(gerundio)
Present Participle: *haciendo*

Past Participle: *hecho*

Singular	**Plural**	**Singular**	**Plural**
Present Indicative		Present Perfect Indicative	
hago	*hacemos*	*he hecho*	*hemos hecho*
haces	*hacéis*	*has hecho*	*habéis hecho*
hace	*hacen*	*ha hecho*	*han hecho*
Imperfect Indicative		Pluperfect OR Past Perfect Indicative	
hacía	*hacíamos*	*había hecho*	*habíamos hecho*
hacías	*hacíais*	*habías hecho*	*habíais hecho*
hacía	*hacían*	*había hecho*	*habían hecho*
Preterit		Past Anterior OR Preterit Perfect	
hice	*hicimos*	*hube hecho*	*hubimos hecho*
hiciste	*hicisteis*	*hubiste hecho*	*hubisteis hecho*
hizo	*hicieron*	*hubo hecho*	*hubieron hecho*
Future		Future Perfect OR Future Anterior	
haré	*haremos*	*habré hecho*	*habremos hecho*
harás	*haréis*	*habrás hecho*	*habréis hecho*
hará	*harán*	*habrá hecho*	*habrán hecho*
Conditional		Conditional Perfect	
haría	*haríamos*	*habría hecho*	*habríamos hecho*
harías	*haríais*	*habrías hecho*	*habríais hecho*
haría	*harían*	*habría hecho*	*habrían hecho*
Present Subjunctive		Present Perfect OR Past Subjunctive	
haga	*hagamos*	*haya hecho*	*hayamos hecho*
hagas	*hagáis*	*hayas hecho*	*hayáis hecho*
haga	*hagan*	*haya hecho*	*hayan hecho*
Imperfect Subjunctive		Pluperfect OR Past Perfect Subjunctive	
hiciera	*hiciéramos*	*hubiera hecho*	*hubiéramos hecho*
hicieras	*hicierais*	*hubieras hecho*	*hubierais hecho*
hiciera	*hicieran*	*hubiera hecho*	*hubieran hecho*
OR		OR	
hiciese	*hiciésemos*	*hubiese hecho*	*hubiésemos hecho*
hicieses	*hicieseis*	*hubieses hecho*	*hubieseis hecho*
hiciese	*hiciesen*	*hubiese hecho*	*hubiesen hecho*

Imperative

—	*hagamos*
haz; no hagas	*haced; no hagáis*
haga	*hagan*

ir / to go

(gerundio)
Present Participle: *yendo*   Past Participle: *ido*

Singular	**Plural**	**Singular**	**Plural**

Present Indicative

voy	*vamos*	
vas	*vais*	
va	*van*	

Present Perfect Indicative

he ido	*hemos ido*
has ido	*habéis ido*
ha ido	*han ido*

Imperfect Indicative

iba	*íbamos*
ibas	*ibais*
iba	*iban*

Pluperfect OR Past Perfect Indicative

había ido	*habíamos ido*
habías ido	*habíais ido*
había ido	*habían ido*

Preterit

fui	*fuimos*
fuiste	*fuisteis*
fue	*fueron*

Past Anterior OR Preterit Perfect

hube ido	*hubimos ido*
hubiste ido	*hubisteis ido*
hubo ido	*hubieron ido*

Future

iré	*iremos*
irás	*iréis*
irá	*irán*

Future Perfect OR Future Anterior

habré ido	*habremos ido*
habrás ido	*habréis ido*
habrá ido	*habrán ido*

Conditional

iría	*iríamos*
irías	*iríais*
iría	*irían*

Conditional Perfect

habría ido	*habríamos ido*
habrías ido	*habríais ido*
habría ido	*habrían ido*

Present Subjunctive

vaya	*vayamos*
vayas	*vayáis*
vaya	*vayan*

Present Perfect OR Past Subjunctive

haya ido	*hayamos ido*
hayas ido	*hayáis ido*
haya ido	*hayan ido*

Imperfect Subjunctive

fuera	*fuéramos*
fueras	*fuerais*
fuera	*fueran*

Pluperfect OR Past Perfect Subjunctive

hubiera ido	*hubiéramos ido*
hubieras ido	*hubierais ido*
hubiera ido	*hubieran ido*

OR

fuese	*fuésemos*
fueses	*fueseis*
fuese	*fuesen*

OR

hubiese ido	*hubiésemos ido*
hubieses ido	*hubieseis ido*
hubiese ido	*hubiesen ido*

Imperative

—	*vamos (no vayamos)*
ve; no vayas	*id; no vayáis*
vaya	*vayan*

ser / to be

(gerundio)

Present Participle: *siendo*		Past Participle: *sido*	
Singular	**Plural**	**Singular**	**Plural**
Present Indicative		Present Perfect Indicative	
soy	*somos*	*he sido*	*hemos sido*
eres	*sois*	*has sido*	*habéis sido*
es	*son*	*ha sido*	*han sido*
Imperfect Indicative		Pluperfect OR Past Perfect Indicative	
era	*éramos*	*había sido*	*habíamos sido*
eras	*erais*	*habías sido*	*habíais sido*
era	*eran*	*había sido*	*habían sido*
Preterit		Past Anterior OR Preterit Perfect	
fui	*fuimos*	*hube sido*	*hubimos sido*
fuiste	*fuisteis*	*hubiste sido*	*hubisteis sido*
fue	*fueron*	*hubo sido*	*hubieron sido*
Future		Future Perfect OR Future Anterior	
seré	*seremos*	*habré sido*	*habremos sido*
serás	*seréis*	*habrás sido*	*habréis sido*
será	*serán*	*habrá sido*	*habrán sido*
Conditional		Conditional Perfect	
sería	*seríamos*	*habría sido*	*habríamos sido*
serías	*seríais*	*habrías sido*	*habríais sido*
sería	*serían*	*habría sido*	*habrían sido*
Present Subjunctive		Present Perfect OR Past Subjunctive	
sea	*seamos*	*haya sido*	*hayamos sido*
seas	*seáis*	*hayas sido*	*hayáis sido*
sea	*sean*	*haya sido*	*hayan sido*
Imperfect Subjunctive		Pluperfect OR Past Perfect Subjunctive	
fuera	*fuéramos*	*hubiera sido*	*hubiéramos sido*
fueras	*fuerais*	*hubieras sido*	*hubierais sido*
fuera	*fueran*	*hubiera sido*	*hubieran sido*
OR		OR	
fuese	*fuésemos*	*hubiese sido*	*hubiésemos sido*
fueses	*fueseis*	*hubieses sido*	*hubieseis sido*
fuese	*fuesen*	*hubiese sido*	*hubiesen sido*

Imperative

—	*seamos*
sé; no seas	*sed; no seáis*
sea	*sean*

§7.8 INFINITIVES

Definition

In English, an infinitive is identified as a verb with the preposition "to" in front of it: to talk, to eat, to live. In Spanish, an infinitive is identified by its ending, those that end in *-ar*, *-er*, *-ir*: *hablar* (to talk, to speak), *comer* (to eat), *vivir* (to live).

§7.8–1 Negation

To make an infinitive negative, place *no* in front of it.

> *No entrar.* / Do not enter.

§7.8–2 Verbal Nouns

A verbal noun is a verb used as a noun. In Spanish, an infinitive may be used as a noun. This means that an infinitive may be used as a subject, a direct object, a predicate noun, or object of a preposition.

● As a subject:

> *Ser o no ser es la cuestión.* / To be or not to be is the question.
> *El estudiar es bueno.* OR *Estudiar es bueno.* / Studying (to study) is good.

Here, when the infinitive is a subject and it begins the sentence, you may use the definite article *el* in front of the infinitive or you may omit it.

If the sentence does not begin with the infinitive, do not use the definite article *el* in front of it:

> *Es bueno estudiar.* / It is good to study.

• As a direct object:

> *No deseo comer.* / I do not want to eat.

• As a predicate noun:

> *Ver es creer.* / Seeing is believing (To see is to believe).

• As object of a preposition:

> *después de llegar* / after arriving

Here, the infinitive (verbal noun) *llegar* is object of the preposition *de*.

In Spanish, an infinitive is ordinarily used after such verbs as *dejar*, *hacer*, *mandar*, and *permitir* with no preposition needed:

> *Luis dejó caer sus libros.* / Louis dropped his books.
>
> *Mi madre me hizo leerlo.* / My mother made me read it.
>
> *Mi profesor me permitió hacerlo.* / My teacher permitted me to do it.

Note that when *dejar* is followed by the preposition *de* it means to stop or to cease:

> *Luis dejó de trabajar.* / Louis stopped working.

The verb *pensar* is directly followed by an infinitive with no preposition required in front of the infinitive when its meaning is "to intend":

> *Pienso ir a Chile.* / I intend to go to Chile.

Ordinarily, the infinitive form of a verb is used right after a preposition:

Antes de estudiar, Rita telefoneó a su amiga Beatriz. / Before
  studying, Rita telephoned her friend Beatrice.
El mimo salió de la sala sin decir nada. / The mime left the room
  without saying anything.

The infinitive form of a verb is ordinarily used after certain
verbs of perception, such as *ver* and *oír*:

Las vi salir. / I saw them go out.
Las oí cantar. / I heard them singing.

After *al*, a verb is used in the infinitive form:

Al entrar en la escuela, Dorotea fue a su clase de español. / Upon
  entering the school, Dorothy went to her Spanish class.

The perfect infinitive (also known as the past infinitive) is
formed by using *haber* in its infinitive form + the past participle
of the main verb:

haber hablado / to have spoken
haber comido / to have eaten
haber escrito / to have written

Summary of verb tenses and moods in Spanish with English equivalents

Los siete tiempos simples
The seven simple tenses

Los siete tiempos compuestos
The seven compound tenses

Tense No.	Tense Name	Tense No.	Tense Name
1	**Present de indicativo** *Present indicative*	8	**Perfecto de indicativo** *Present perfect indicative*
2	**Imperfecto de indicativo** *Imperfect indicative*	9	**Pluscuamperfecto de indicativo** *Pluperfect or Past perfect indicative*
3	**Pretérito** *Preterit*	10	**Pretérito anterior (Pret. perfecto)** *Past anterior or Preterit perfect*
4	**Futuro** *Future*	11	**Futuro perfecto** *Future perfect or Future anterior*
5	**Potencial simple** *Conditional*	12	**Potencial compuesto** *Conditional perfect*
6	**Presente de subjuntivo** *Present subjunctive*	13	**Perfecto de subjuntivo** *Present perfect or Past subjunctive*
7	**Imperfecto de subjuntivo** *Imperfect subjunctive*	14	**Pluscuamperfecto de subjuntivo** *Pluperfect or Past perfect subjunctive*

The imperative is not a tense; it is a mood.

§8.

Adverbs: Beginner, Intermediate, and Advanced Levels

DEFINITION

An adverb is a word that modifies a verb, an adjective, or another adverb.

§8.1 FORMATION

An adverb is regularly formed by adding the ending *-mente* to the feminine singular form of an adjective.

> *lento, lenta / lentamente:* slow / slowly
> *rápido, rápida / rápidamente:* rapid / rapidly

If the form of the adjective is the same for the feminine singular and masculine singular (*fácil, feliz*), add *-mente* to that form.

> *fácil* (easy) / *fácilmente* (easily)
> *feliz* (happy) / *felizmente* (happily)

Note that an accent mark on an adjective remains when the adjective is changed to an adverb. And note that the Spanish ending *-mente* is equivalent to the ending -ly in English.

An adverb remains invariable; that is to say, it does not agree in gender and number and therefore does not change in form.

There are many adverbs that do not end in *-mente*. Some common ones are:

abajo / below	*arriba* / above
bien / well	*mal* / badly
hoy / today	*mañana* / tomorrow
siempre / always	*nunca* / never
aquí / here	*allí* / there

Tip

The adverbial ending *ísimo*
Never use *muy* in front of *mucho*. Say *muchísimo*:

> *Elena trabaja muchísimo.* / Helen works a great deal; Helen works very, very much.

§8.2 COMPARISON

Regular comparison of adverbs

An adverb is compared regularly as an adjective.

> *María corre tan rápidamente como Elena.* / Mary runs as rapidly as Helen.
> *María corre menos rápidamente que Anita.* / Mary runs less rapidly than Anita.
> *María corre más rápidamente que Isabel.* / Mary runs more rapidly than Isabel.

Irregular comparative adverbs

mucho, poco / much, little: *Roberto trabaja mucho; Felipe trabaja poco.*
bien, mal / well, badly: *Juan trabaja bien; Lucas trabaja mal.*
más, menos / more, less: *Carlota trabaja más que Casandra; Elena trabaja menos que Marta.*
mejor, peor / better, worse: *Paula trabaja mejor que Anita; Isabel trabaja peor que Elena.*

§8.3 COMMONLY USED INTERROGATIVE ADVERBS

Some common interrogative adverbs are:

¿cómo? / how? *¿cuándo?* / when?
¿cuánto?, ¿cuánta?, ¿cuántos?, ¿cuántas? / how much?
   how many?
¿por qué? / why? *¿para qué?* / why? *¿dónde?* / where?
¿adónde? / where to? (to where?)

§8.4 COMMONLY USED NEGATIVE ADVERBS

jamás / ever, never, not ever
nada / nothing (*sin nada* / without anything); after *sin*,
   nada is used instead of *algo*:
Ella no quiere nada. / She does not want anything.

ni / neither, nor	*también* / also, too
ni . . . ni / neither . . . nor	*tampoco* / neither
ni siquiera / not even	*ni yo tampoco* / nor I either
nunca / never, not ever,	*unos cuantos, unas cuantas* /
ever	a few, some, several
siempre / always	

No había criatura que se movía, ni siquiera un ratón. / Not
a creature was stirring, not even a mouse.

§8.5 SPECIAL USES

§8.5–1 Adverbs Replaced by Adjectives

An adverb may sometimes be replaced by an adjective whose
agreement is with the subject, especially if the verb is one of
motion:

   Las muchachas van y vienen silenciosas. / The girls come and go
   silently.

§8.5–2 *Ahí, allí, allá*

These three adverbs all mean "there" but they have special uses:

- *Ahí* means there, not too far away from the person who says it:

    El libro que Ud. quiere está ahí sobre esa mesa. / The book that you want is there on that table.

- *Allí* means there, farther away from the person who says it, or even at a remote distance:

    ¿Quiere Ud. ir a Chicago? Sí, porque mi padre trabaja allí. / Do you want to go to Chicago? Yes, because my father works there.

- *Allá* means there, generally used with a verb of motion:

    Me gustaría mucho ir allá. / I would like very much to go there.
    Bueno, ¡vaya allá! / Good, go there!

§8.5–3 *Aquí* and *acá*

These two adverbs both mean "here" but they have special uses:

- *Aquí* means here, a place close to the person who says it:

    Aquí se habla español. / Spanish is spoken here.

- *Acá* means here, a place close to the person who says it, but it is used with a verb of motion:

    Señor Gómez, ¡venga acá, por favor! / Mr. Gómez, come here, please!

§8.5–4 *Con, sin* + noun

At times, an adverb can be formed by using the preposition *con* (with) or *sin* (without) + a noun:

con cuidado / carefully	*con dificultad* / with difficulty
sin cuidado / carelessly	*sin dificultad* / without difficulty

The adverb *recientemente* (recently) becomes *recién* before a past participle:

> *los recién llegados* / the ones recently arrived; the recently arrived (ones)

§9.

Prepositions: Beginner, Intermediate, and Advanced Levels

DEFINITION

A preposition is a word that connects words and, according to the thought expressed in the sentence, serves to indicate the relationship between the words.

§9.1 COMMON PREPOSITIONS IN SPANISH

a / at, to	*hacia* / toward
ante / before, in the presence of	*hasta* / until, up to, as far as
bajo / under	*menos* / except
con / with	*para* / for, in order to
contra / against	*por* / by, for
de / of, from	*salvo* / except, save
desde / after, from, since	*según* / according to
durante / during	*sin* / without
en / in, on	*sobre* / on, upon, over, above
entre / among, between	*tras* / after, behind

§9.2 COMMON PREPOSITIONAL PHRASES IN SPANISH

acerca de / about	*antes de nada* / before anything
además de / in addition to, besides	*antes de nadie* / before anyone
alrededor de / around	*cerca de* / near
antes de / before	

con rumbo a / in the direction of	*en lugar de* / in place of, instead of
debajo de / underneath	*en medio de* / in the middle of
delante de / in front of	*en vez de* / instead of
dentro de / within, inside (of)	*encima de* / on top of, upon
después de / after	*enfrente de* / opposite
detrás de / in back of, behind	*frente a* / in front of
en contra de / against	*fuera de* / outside of
en cuanto a / as far as	*junto a* / next to
	lejos de / far from
	por valor de / worth

§9.3 DISTINCTION BETWEEN A PREPOSITION AND AN ADVERB

Many prepositional phrases, such as the ones given above, would not be prepositional if the preposition *de* were not included in the phrase; without the preposition *de*, most of them are adverbs.

además / furthermore; *además de* / in addition to
alrededor / around; *alrededor de* / around
debajo / under; *debajo de* / underneath
lejos / far, far off; *lejos de* / far from

The use of the preposition *de* with these adverbs, and others, changes the part of speech to a preposition, as in prepositional phrases such as:

lejos de la escuela / far from the school
alrededor de la casa / around the house

Generally speaking, prepositions require a noun or a pronoun right after them (sometimes an infinitive, as in *sin decir nada* / without saying anything).

§9.4 USES OF PREPOSITIONS

Generally speaking, prepositions are used in the following categories:

> preposition + a noun: *con María* / with Mary;
>   *con mi amigo* / with my friend
> preposition + a pronoun: *para ella* / for her;
>   *para usted* / for you
> preposition + infinitive: *sin hablar* / without talking
> verb + preposition: *gozar de algo* / to enjoy something

§9.5 SPECIAL CASES

§9.5–1 Personal *a*

In Spanish, the preposition *a* is used in front of a person or something that is personified when that person (or personified thing) is the direct object of the verb.

> *Conozco a su hermana Elena.* / I know your sister Helen.
> *¿Conoce Ud. a Roberto?* / Do you know Robert?
> *Llamo al médico.* / I am calling the doctor.

The personal *a* is used in front of an indefinite pronoun when it is the direct object of a verb and it refers to a person, for example: *nadie, ninguno (ninguna), alguien, alguno (alguna), quien:*

> *Mis padres están visitando a alguien en el hospital.* / My parents are visiting someone in the hospital.
> *¿Ve Ud. a alguien?* / Do you see anybody?
> *No veo a nadie.* / I don't see anybody.

The personal *a* is used in front of a geographic name if it is used as direct object:

> *Este verano pensamos visitar a Colombia.* / This summer we plan to visit Colombia.

But if the geographic place contains a definite article in front of it (which is part of its name), the personal *a* is not used:

> *¿Ha visitado Ud. la Argentina?* / Have you visited Argentina?
> *La familia Gómez en Guadalajara quiere visitar los Estados Unidos.* / The Gómez family in Guadalajara wants to visit the United States.

The personal *a* is used in front of a noun that is a domestic animal when it is personified and when it is a direct object:

> *Quiero a mi gatito.* / I love my kitten.

The personal *a* is not generally used with the verb *tener* when it means " to have":

> *Tengo dos hermanas y dos hermanos.* / I have two sisters and two brothers.

But when *tener* means "to hold," the personal *a* is generally used:

> *La enfermera tenía al niño en los brazos.* / The nurse was holding the child in her arms.

§9.5–2 *Para con*

The prepositional expression *para con*, meaning "to" or "toward," in the sense of with respect to or as regards, is used to denote a mental attitude or feeling about a person:

> *Nuestra profesora de español es muy amable para con nosotros.* / Our Spanish teacher is very kind to us.

§9.5–3 *Para* and *por*

These two prepositions are generally translated into English as "for."

Use *para* when you mean:

Destination:

> *Mañana salgo para Madrid.* / Tomorrow I am leaving for Madrid.

Intended for:

> *Este vaso es para María y ese vaso es para José.* / This glass is for Mary, and that glass is for Joseph.
>
> *Esta taza es para café; es una taza para café.* / This cup is for coffee; it is a coffee cup.

Purpose (in order to):

> *Estudio para llegar a ser médico.* / I am studying in order to become a doctor.

A comparison of some sort:

> *Para ser norteamericano, habla español muy bien.* / For an American, he speaks Spanish very well.

At some point in future time:

> *Esta lección es para mañana.* / This lesson is for tomorrow.

Use *por* when you mean:

A length of time:

> *Me quedé en casa por tres días.* / I stayed at home for three days.

In exchange for:

> *¿Cuánto dinero me dará Ud. por mi trabajo?* / How much money will you give me for my work?

To send for:

> *Vamos a enviar por el médico.* / We are going to send for the doctor.

By:

> *Este libro fue escrito por dos autores.* / This book was written by two authors.
>
> *Quiero enviar esta carta por correo.* / I want to send this letter by post.

For the sake of, as an obligation, on someone's behalf:

> *Quiero hacerlo por usted.* / I want to do it for you.
>
> *Por la paz* / For (the sake of) peace.

Through:

> *Dimos un paseo por el parque.* / We took a walk through the park.

Along, by the edge of:

> *Anduvimos por la playa.* / We walked along the beach.

To fight for:

> *Luché por mi amigo.* / I fought for my friend.

Out of, because of + noun:

> *No quisieron hacerlo por miedo.* / They refused to do it out of (for) fear.

Per, when expressing frequency:

> *Los alumnos asisten a la escuela cinco días porsemana.* / Students attend school five days a (per) week.

To go for someone or something:

> *Mi madre fue por Carmen.* / My mother went for (went to get) Carmen.
>
> *Mi madre fue por pan.* / My mother went for (went to get) bread.

To ask about, to inquire about, using *preguntar por*:

> *Pregunto por el médico.* / I am asking for the doctor.

§9.5–4 *Por* or *de*

The preposition *por* is sometimes translated into English as "by," although it has other meanings, such as "through" or "for."

The preposition *de* is sometimes translated into English as "by," and it has other meanings, too, such as "of," "from" or "in."

When using a passive meaning that expresses an action performed by someone or something, *por* is generally used.

Use the preposition *de* to express "by" when using a passive meaning if some emotion or feeling is expressed instead of an action.

> *La señora Gómez es respetada de todos los alumnos.* / Mrs. Gómez is respected by all the students.

§9.5–5 Special Uses of *para* and *por*

¿Para qué . . . ? and *¿Por qué . . . ?*

Both of these interrogatives mean "why," but they are not used interchangeably. If by "why" you mean for what reason, use *¿por qué . . . ?* If by "why" you mean for what purpose (what for?), use *¿para qué . . . ?*

Examples:

> *Juanita, ¿por qué lloras?* / Jeanie, why (for what reason) are you crying?
>
> *Mamá, ¿para qué tengo un ombligo?* / Mom, why (what for, for what purpose) do I have a bellybutton?

§10.
Conjunctions: Beginner, Intermediate, and Advanced Levels

DEFINITION

A conjunction is a word that connects words, phrases, clauses, or sentences.

§10.1 COMMON CONJUNCTIONS

a fin de que / so that, in order that

a menos que / unless

antes (de) que / before

apenas . . . cuando / hardly, scarcely . . . when

así que / as soon as, after

aun / even

aún / still, yet

aunque / although

como / as, since, how

como si / as if

con tal (de) que / provided that

cuando / when

de manera que / so that

de modo que / so that, in such a way that

después (de) que / after

e / and (before *i* or *hi*)

en cuanto / as soon as

hasta que / until

luego que / as soon as, after

mas / but

mas que / even if, however much

mientras / while

mientras que / while, so long as, as long as

ni / neither, nor (*ni . . . ni* / neither . . . nor)

ni siquiera / not even

a condición de que / on condition that

a pesar de que / in spite of

así . . . como / both . . . and

aun cuando / even if

caso que / in case that

como que / it seems that, apparently

como quiera que / although, since

con la condición de que / on condition that

dado caso que / supposing that

dado que / supposing that

de condición que / so as to

de suerte que / so that, in such a manner as

desde que / since

empero / yet, however, notwithstanding

These conjunctions may be less familiar to you:

y, pero, o, porque / and, but, or, because

ni sólo . . . (sino) también / not only . . . but also

o / or (*o . . . o* / either . . . or)

o sea . . . o sea / either . . . or

para que / in order that, so that

pero / but

por cuanto / inasmuch as

porque / because

pues que / since

puesto que / although, since, inasmuch as, as long as

que / that, because

según que / depending on

si / if, whether

sin embargo / nevertheless, notwithstanding, however (in whatever way)

sin que / without

sino / but, but rather

sino que / but that, but rather that

siquiera / though, although, whether, or

tan pronto como / as soon as

u / or (before *o* or *ho*)

y / and

ya . . . ya / now . . . now

ya que / since, seeing that

en caso de que / in case, in case that

en razón de que / for the reason that

entretanto que / meanwhile, while

más bien que / rather than

mientras tanto / meanwhile

no bien . . . cuando / no sooner . . . than

por más que / no matter how, however much

por razón de que / for the reason that

salvo que / unless

siempre que / whenever, provided that

tan luego como / therefore

tanto . . . como / as much . . . as

§10.2 OTHER CONJUNCTIONS

§10.2–1 *Pero* and *sino*

These two words are conjunctions and they both mean "but."
Note the uses:

> *Me gustaría venir a tu casa esta noche pero no puedo.* / I would
> like to come to your house tonight, but I can't.

Use *sino* to mean "but rather" or "but on the contrary":

> *Pedro no es pequeño sino alto.* / Peter is not short
> but tall.
> *Mi automóvil no es amarillo sino blanco.* / My car is not yellow
> but white.

Note that when you use *sino* the first part of the sentence
is negative. Also note that *sino* may be followed by an
infinitive:

> *Pablo no quiere alquilar el automóvil sino comprarlo.* / Paul does
> not want to rent the car but to buy it.

If a clause follows *sino*, use *sino que*:

> *Pablo no alquiló el automóvil sino que lo compró.* / Paul did not
> rent the car but bought it.

And note finally that *sino* is used instead of *pero* when you
make a clear contrast between a negative thought in the first
part of the sentence and a positive thought in the second
part. If no contrast is made or intended, use *pero*:

> *María no conoce al niño pero le habla.* / Mary does not know the
> child but talks to him.

§10.2–2 *Pero* and *mas*

These two words are conjunctions, and they both mean
"but." In plays and poems an author may sometimes
use *mas* instead of *pero*. In conversation and informal
writing, *pero* is used. Note that *mas* with no accent mark
means "but" and *más* (with the accent mark) means
"more."

§10.2–3 O and *u*

These two words, which are conjunctions, mean "or." Use *o* normally, but when a word that is right after *o* begins with *o* or *ho*, use *u*:

> *muchachos u hombres* / boys or men; *septiembre u octubre* /
> September or October

§10.2–4 Y and *e*

These two words, which are conjunctions, mean "and." Use *y* normally but when a word that is right after *y* begins with *i* or *hi*, use *e*:

> *María es bonita e inteligente.* / Mary is pretty and intelligent.
> *Fernando e Isabel* / Ferdinand and Isabel
> *madre e hija* / mother and daughter
> *padre e hijo* / father and son

However, if *y* is followed by a word that begins with *hie*, keep *y*:

> *flores y hierba* / flowers and grass

Special Topics
Beginner, Intermediate, and Advanced Levels

§11.

Exclamatory Statements
¡Qué . . . ! and *¡Tal . . . !*

In English, when we exclaim "What a class!"; "What a student!"; "What an idea!"; or "Such an idea!"; we use the indefinite article *a* or *an*. In Spanish, however, we do not use the indefinite article.

> *¡Qué clase! ¡Qué alumno! ¡Qué alumna! ¡Qué idea!* OR *¡Tal idea!*

If an adjective is used to describe the noun, we generally use *más* or *tan* in front of the adjective, in order to intensify the exclamation.

> *¡Qué chica tan bonita!* / What a pretty girl!
> *¡Qué libro más interesante!* / What an interesting book!

When we use *¡Qué!* + an adjective, the meaning in English is "How . . . !"

> *¡Qué difícil es!* / How difficult it is!

§12.
Idioms

§12.1 SPECIAL PHRASES

¿Cuánto tiempo hace que + present tense . . . ?

Use the present tense of the verb when the action of studying, waiting, etc. is still going on at the present.

> ¿Cuánto tiempo hace que Ud. estudia español? / How long have you been studying Spanish?
>
> ¿Cuánto tiempo hace que Ud. espera el autobús? / How long have you been waiting for the bus?

¿Cuánto tiempo hacía que + imperfect tense . . . ?

If the action of the verb began in the past and ended in the past, use the imperfect tense.

> ¿Cuánto tiempo hacía que Ud. hablaba cuando yo entré en la sala de clase? / How long had you been talking when I entered the classroom?

¿Desde cuándo + present tense . . . ?

This is another way of asking: How long (since when) + the present perfect tense in English, as given above.

> ¿Desde cuándo estudia Ud. español? / How long have you been studying Spanish?

Present tense + desde hace + length of time

> Estudio español desde hace tres años. / I have been studying Spanish for three years.

¿Desde cuándo + imperfect tense . . . ?

¿Desde cuándo hablaba Ud. cuando yo entré en la sala de clase? / How long had you been talking when I entered the classroom?

Imperfect tense + desde hacía + length of time

(Yo) hablaba desde hacía una hora cuando Ud. entró en la sala de clase. / I had been talking for one hour when you entered the classroom.

Hace + length of time + que + present tense

Hace tres años que estudio español. / I have been studying Spanish for three years.

Hace veinte minutos que espero el autobús. / I have been waiting for the bus for twenty minutes.

¿Cuántos años hace que Ud. estudia español? / How many years have you been studying Spanish?

¿Cuántas horas hace que Ud. mira la televisión? / How many hours have you been watching television?

Hacía + length of time + que + imperfect tense

Hacía una hora que yo hablaba cuando Ud. entró en sala de clase. / I had been talking for one hour when you entered the classroom.

Hay and *hay que* + infinitive

The word *hay* is not a verb; it is a form of *haber*. Its English equivalent is: There is . . . or There are . . .

> *Hay muchos libros en la mesa.* / There are many books on the table.
> *Hay una mosca en la sopa.* / There is a fly in the soup.

Hay que + infinitive is an impersonal expression that denotes an obligation, and it is commonly translated into English as: One must . . . or It is necessary to . . .

> *Hay que estudiar para aprender.* / It is necessary to study in order to learn.

Medio and *mitad*

Both these words mean "half," but they are used in different ways:

Medio is an adjective, and it agrees with the noun it modifies:

> *Necesito media docena de huevos.* / I need half a dozen eggs.
> *Llegaremos en media hora.* / We will arrive in a half hour (in half an hour).

Medio is also used as an adverb:

> *Los caballos corrieron rápidamente y ahora están medio muertos.* / The horses ran fast, and now they are half dead.

Mitad is a feminine noun:

> *El alumno estudió la mitad de la lección.* / The pupil studied half (of) the lesson.

§12.2 COMMON EXPRESSIONS

---

with *a*

---

a bordo / on board
a caballo / on horseback

a cada instante / at every moment, at every turn

a casa / home (Use with a verb of motion; use *a casa* if you are going to the house; use *en casa* if you are in the house.)

a eso de / about, around

> *Llegaremos a Madrid a eso de las tres de la tarde.* / We will arrive in Madrid at about 3 o'clock in the afternoon.

a fines de / about the end of, around the end of

> *Estaremos en Madrid a fines de la semana.* / We will be in Madrid around the end of the week.

a mano / by hand

a mediados de / around the middle of

> *Estaremos en Málaga a mediados de julio.* / We will be in Málaga around the middle of July.

a menudo / often, frequently

a mi parecer / in my opinion

a pesar de / in spite of

a pie / on foot

a principios de / around the beginning of

> *Estaremos en México a principios de la semana que viene.* / We will be in Mexico around the beginning of next week.

a saltos / by leaps and bounds

a tiempo / on time

a través de / across, through

a veces / at times, sometimes

a vuelo de pájaro / as the crow flies

estar a punto de / to be about to

> *Estoy a punto de salir.* / I am about to leave.

frente a / in front of

junto a / beside, next to

poco a poco / little by little

ser aficionado a / to be a fan of

uno a uno / one by one

with *a la*

a la derecha / to (on, at) the right
a la española / in the Spanish style
a la francesa / in the French style
a la italiana / in the Italian style
a la izquierda / to (on, at) the left
a la larga / in the long run
a la madrugada / at an early hour, at daybreak
a la semana / a week, per week
a la vez / at the same time

with *al*

al + infinitive / on, upon + present participle

> *Al entrar en la cocina, comenzó a comer.* / Upon entering the kitchen, he began to eat.

al aire libre / outdoors, in the open air
al amanecer / at daybreak, at dawn
al anochecer / at nightfall, at dusk
al cabo / finally, at last
al cabo de / at the end of
al contrario / on the contrary
al día / current, up to date
al día siguiente / on the following day, on the next day
al fin / at last, finally
al lado de / next to, beside
al menos / at least
al mes / a month, per month
al parecer / apparently
al principio / at first
echar al correo / to mail a letter

with *con*

con frecuencia / frequently
con los brazos abiertos / with open arms
con motivo de / because of, on the occasion of
con mucho gusto / gladly, willingly, with much pleasure
con permiso / excuse me, with your permission
con rumbo a / in the direction of
ser amable con / to be kind to

with *cuanto, cuanta, cuantos, cuantas*

cuanto antes / as soon as possible
¿Cuánto cuesta? / How much is it? How much does it cost?
cuanto más . . . tanto más . . . / the more . . . the more . . .

> *Cuanto más estudio tanto más aprendo.* / The more I study the more I learn.

¿Cuántos años tiene Ud.? / How old are you?
unos cuantos libros / a few books
unas cuantas flores / a few flowers

with *dar* and *darse*

dar a / to face, to look out on

> *El comedor da al jardín.* / The dining room faces the garden.

dar con algo / to find something, to come upon something

> *Esta mañana di con dinero en la calle.* / This morning I found money in the street.

dar con alguien / to meet someone, to run into someone, to come across someone, to find someone

> *Anoche, di con mi amiga Elena en el cine.* / Last night I met my friend Helen at the movies.

dar contra / to hit against

dar de beber a / to give something to drink to

dar de comer a / to feed, to give something to eat to

> *Me gusta dar de comer a los pájaros en el parque.* / I like to feed the birds in the park.

dar en / to hit against, to strike against

dar la bienvenida / to welcome

dar la hora / to strike the hour

dar la mano a alguien / to shake hands with someone

dar las gracias a alguien / to thank someone

dar los buenos días a alguien / to say good morning (hello) to someone

dar por + past participle / to consider

> *Lo doy por perdido.* / I consider it lost.

dar recuerdos a / to give one's regards (best wishes) to

dar un abrazo / to embrace

dar un paseo / to take a walk

dar un paseo a caballo / to go horseback riding

dar un paseo en automóvil (en coche) / to go for a drive

dar un paseo en bicicleta / to ride a bicycle

dar una vuelta / to go for a short walk, to go for a stroll

dar unas palmadas / to clap one's hands

dar voces / to shout

darse cuenta de / to realize, to be aware of, to take into account

darse la mano / to shake hands with each other

darse prisa / to hurry

---

with *de*

acabar de + infinitive / to have just + past participle

> *María acaba de llegar.* / Mary has just arrived.
> *María acababa de llegar.* / Mary had just arrived.

acerca de / about, concerning

alrededor de / around

alrededor de la casa / around the house

antes de / before

aparte de / aside from

billete de ida y vuelta / round-trip ticket

cerca de / near, close to

de abajo / down, below

de acuerdo / in agreement, in accord

de aquí en adelante / from now on

de arriba / upstairs

de arriba abajo / from top to bottom

de ayer en ocho días / a week from yesterday

de balde / free, gratis

de broma / jokingly

de buena gana / willingly

de cuando en cuando / from time to time

de día / by day, in the daytime

de día en día / from day to day

de esa manera / in that way

de ese modo / in that way

de esta manera / in this way

de este modo / in this way

de hoy en adelante / from today on, from now on

de hoy en ocho días / a week from today

de la mañana / in the morning (Use this when a specific time is mentioned.)

> *Tomo el desayuno a las ocho de la mañana.* / I have breakfast at 8 o'clock in the morning.

de la noche / in the evening (Use this when a specific time is mentioned.)

> *Mi amigo llega a las nueve de la noche.* / My friend is arriving at 9 o'clock in the evening.

de la tarde / in the afternoon (Use this when a specific time is mentioned.)

> *Regreso a casa a las cuatro de la tarde.* / I am returning home at 4 o'clock in the afternoon.

de madrugada / at dawn, at daybreak
de mal humor / in bad humor, in a bad mood
de mala gana / unwillingly
de memoria / by heart (memorized)
de moda / in fashion
de nada / you're welcome
de ningún modo / no way, in no way, by no means
de ninguna manera / no way, in no way, by no means
de noche / by night, at night, during the night
de nuevo / again
de otra manera / in another way
de otro modo / otherwise
de pie / standing
de prisa / in a hurry
de pronto / suddenly
de repente / all of a sudden
de rodillas / kneeling, on one's knees
de todos modos / anyway, in any case, at any rate
de uno en uno / one by one
de veras / really, truly
de vez en cuando / from time to time
ir de compras / to go shopping
no hay de qué / you're welcome, don't mention it
un poco de / a little (of)
un poco de azúcar / a little sugar

with *decir*

decirle al oído / to whisper in one's ear
dicho y hecho / no sooner said than done
Es decir . . . / That is to say . . .
querer decir / to mean

> *¿Qué quiere decir este palabra?* / What does this word mean?

with *día, días*

al día / current, up to date
al romper el día / at daybreak
algún día / someday
de día en día / day by day
día por día / day by day
estar al día / to be up to date
hoy día / nowadays
por día / by the day, per day
quince días / two weeks
un día de éstos / one of these days

with *en*

en bicicleta / by bicycle
en broma / jokingly, in fun
en cambio / on the other hand
en casa / at home (Use *en casa* if you are in the house;
   use *a casa* with a verb of motion, if you are going to the
   house.)

> *Me quedo en casa esta noche.* / I am staying home tonight.
> *Salgo de la escuela y voy a casa.* / I'm leaving school, and I'm
>   going home.

en casa de / at the house of

> *María está en casa de Elena.* / Mary is at Helen's house.

en caso de / in case of
en coche / by car
en cuanto / as soon as
en cuanto a / as for, with regard to, in regard to
en efecto / as a matter of fact, in fact
en este momento / at this moment
en lo alto de / on top of, at the top of, up
en lugar de / in place of, instead of

en *medio de* / in the middle of
en *ninguna parte* / nowhere
en *punto* / sharp, exactly (telling time)

> *Son las dos en punto.* / It is two o'clock sharp.

en *seguida* / immediately, at once
en *todas partes* / everywhere
en *vano* / in vain
en *vez de* / instead of
en *voz alta* / in a loud voice
en *voz baja* / in a low voice

---

with *estar*

está bien / all right, okay
estar a punto de + infinitive / to be about + infinitive

> *Estoy a punto de salir.* / I am about to go out.

estar conforme con / to be in agreement with
estar de acuerdo / to agree
estar de acuerdo con / to be in agreement with
estar en boga / to be in fashion, in vogue
estar de buenas / to be in a good mood
estar de moda / to be in fashion
estar de pie / to be standing
estar de vuelta / on the way
estar para + infinitive / to be about to

> *Estoy para salir.* / I am about to go out.

estar por / to be in favor of
no estar para bromas / not to be in the mood for jokes

---

with *haber*

ha habido . . . / there has been . . . , there have been . . .
había . . . / there was . . . , there were . . .

habrá . . . / there will be . . .
habría . . . / there would be . . .
hubo . . . / there was . . . , there were . . .

---

with *hacer* and *hacerse*

---

hace poco / a little while ago
hace un año / a year ago

> *Hace un mes que partió el señor Molina.* / Mr. Molina left one month ago.

hacer daño a alguien / to harm someone
hacer de un camino dos mandados / to kill two birds with one stone (*un mandado* / an errand)
hacer la maleta / to pack one's suitcase
hacer el baúl / to pack one's trunk
hacer el favor de + infinitive / please

> *Haga Ud. el favor de entrar.* / Please come in.

hacer el papel de / to play the role of
hacer falta / to be wanting, lacking, needed
Hace falta tener cuidado. / Care must be taken. One must be careful.
hacer pedazos / to smash, to break, to tear into pieces
hacer un viaje / to take a trip
hacer una broma / to play a joke
hacer una pregunta / to ask a question
hacer una visita / to pay a visit
hacerle falta / to need

> *A Juan le hace falta un lápiz.* / John needs a pencil.

hacerse / to become

> *Elena se hizo dentista.* / Helen became a dentist.

hacerse daño / to hurt oneself, to harm oneself
hacerse tarde / to be getting late

> *Vámonos; se hace tarde.* / Let's leave; it's getting late.

with *hasta*

hasta ahora / until now
hasta aquí / until now, up to here
hasta después / see you later, until later
hasta entonces / see you then, see you later, up to that time,
   until that time
hasta la vista / see you again
hasta luego / see you later, until later
hasta mañana / see you tomorrow, until tomorrow

with *lo*

a lo largo de / along
a lo lejos / in the distance
a lo menos / at least
lo bueno / what is good, the good part

> ¡Lo bueno que es! / How good it is!
> ¡Lo bien que está escrito! / How well it is written!

lo de + infinitive, adverb, or noun / "that matter of . . .", "that
   business of . . ."
lo escrito / what is written
lo malo / what is bad, the bad part
lo más pronto posible / as soon as possible
lo mejor / what is best, the best part
lo primero que debo decir / the first thing I must say
lo simpático / whatever is kind, nice
por lo contrario / on the contrary
por lo menos / at least
por lo pronto / in the meantime, for the time being
¡Ya lo creo! / I should certainly think so!

with *luego*

desde luego / naturally, of course, immediately
hasta luego / see you later, so long
luego luego / right away
luego que / as soon as, after

with *mañana*

ayer por la mañana / yesterday morning
de la mañana / in the morning (Use this when a specific time is mentioned.):

> *Voy a tomar el tren a las seis de la mañana.* / I am going to take the train at six o'clock in the morning.

mañana por la mañana / tomorrow morning
mañana por la noche / tomorrow night
mañana por la tarde / tomorrow afternoon
pasado mañana / the day after tomorrow
por la mañana / in the morning (Use this when no exact time is mentioned.):

> *El señor Pardo llega por la mañana.* / Mr. Pardo is arriving in the morning.

por la mañana temprano / early in the morning

with *mismo*

ahora mismo / right now
al mismo tiempo / at the same time
allá mismo / right there
aquí mismo / right here
así mismo / the same, the same thing
el mismo de siempre / the same old thing

eso mismo / that very thing
hoy mismo / this very day
lo mismo / the same, the same thing
lo mismo da / it makes no difference, it amounts to the same thing
lo mismo de siempre / the same old story
lo mismo que / the same as, as well as
por lo mismo / for the same reason

with *no*

Creo que no. / I don't think so, I think not.
No es verdad. / It isn't so, It isn't true;
¿No es verdad? / Isn't that so?
No hay de qué. / You're welcome.
No hay remedio. / There's no way. It cannot be helped.
No importa. / It doesn't matter.
No + verb + *más que* + amount of money

> *No tengo más que un dólar.* / I have only one dollar.

todavía no / not yet
ya no / no longer

with *para*

estar para + infinitive / to be about to, to be at the point of

> *El autobús está para salir.* / The bus is about to leave.

para con / to, toward

> *Nuestra profesora de español es muy amable para con nosotros.* / Our Spanish teacher is very kind to us.

para eso / for that matter
para mí / for my part
para que / in order that, so that

para ser / in spite of being

> *Para ser tan viejo, él es muy ágil.* / In spite of being so old, he is very agile.

para siempre / forever

un vaso para agua / a water glass; *una taza para café* / a coffee cup

---

with *poco*

a poco / in a short while, presently

dentro de poco / in a short while, in a little while

en pocos días / in a few days

poco a poco / little by little

poco antes / shortly before

poco después / shortly after

por poco / nearly, almost

un poco de / a little (of)

> *Quisiera un poco de azúcar.* / I would like a little sugar.

---

with *por*

acabar por + infinitive / to (finally) end up (by) + present participle

> *Mi padre acabó por comprarlo.* / My father finally ended up (by) buying it.

al por mayor / wholesale

al por menor / retail (sales)

ayer por la mañana / yesterday morning

ayer por la noche / yesterday evening

ayer por la tarde / yesterday afternoon

estar por / to be in favor of

mañana por la mañana / tomorrow morning

mañana por la noche / tomorrow night, tomorrow evening

mañana por la tarde / tomorrow afternoon

por ahora / for just now, for the present
por aquí / this way, around here
por avión / by air mail
por consiguiente / consequently
por desgracia / unfortunately
por Dios / for God's sake
por ejemplo / for example
por el contrario OR *por lo contrario* / on the contrary
por escrito / in writing
por eso / for that reason, therefore
por favor / please

> *Entre, por favor.* / Come in, please.

por fin / at last, finally
por hora / by the hour, per hour
por la mañana / in the morning
por la noche / in the evening
por la noche temprano / early in the evening
por la tarde / in the afternoon
por lo común / commonly, generally, usually
por lo general / generally, usually
por lo menos / at least
por lo tanto / consequently, therefore
por lo visto / apparently
por mi parte / as for me, as far as I am concerned
por poco / nearly, almost
por semana / by the week, per week
por supuesto / of course
por teléfono / by phone
por todas partes / everywhere

---

with *pronto*

al pronto / at first
de pronto / suddenly
lo más pronto posible / as soon as possible
por de pronto / for the time being

por el pronto OR *por lo pronto* / in the meantime, for the time being

tan pronto como / as soon as

---

with *que*

Creo que no. / I don't think so, I think not.

Creo que sí. / I think so.

el año que viene / next year

la semana que viene / next week

¡Qué lástima! / What a pity!

¡Qué le vaya bien! / Good luck!

¡Qué lo pase Ud. bien! / Good luck! (I wish you a good outcome!)

---

with *ser*

Debe de ser . . . / It is probably . . .

Debe ser . . . / It ought to be . . .

Es de mi agrado. / It's to my liking.

Es hora de . . . / It is time to . . .

Es lástima. OR *Es una lástima.* / It's a pity; It's too bad.

Es que . . . / The fact is . . .

para ser / in spite of being

> *Para ser tan pobre, Marisol es muy generosa.* / In spite of being so poor, Marisol is very generous.

sea lo que sea / whatever it may be, be that as it may

ser aficionado a / to be a fan of

> *Soy aficionado al béisbol.* / I'm a baseball fan.

ser amable con / to be kind to

> *Mi profesora de español es amable conmigo.* / My Spanish teacher is kind to me.

ser todo oídos / to be all ears

> *Te escucho; soy todo oídos.* / I'm listening to you; I'm all ears.

with *sin*

sin aliento / out of breath
sin cuidado / carelessly
sin duda / without a doubt, undoubtedly, doubtless
sin ejemplo / unparalleled, nothing like it
sin embargo / nevertheless, however
sin falta / without fail
sin novedad / nothing new, same as usual

with *tener*

¿Cuántos años tienes?

> *¿Cuántos años tiene Ud.?* / How old are you?
> *Tengo diez y seis años.* / I am sixteen years old.

¿Qué tienes?

> *¿Qué tiene Ud.?* / What's the matter? What's the matter with you?
> *No tengo nada.* / There's nothing wrong; There's nothing the matter (with me).

tener algo que hacer / to have something to do
tener calor / to feel (to be) warm (persons)
tener cuidado / to be careful
tener dolor de cabeza / to have a headache
tener dolor de estómago / to have a stomachache
tener éxito / to be successful
tener frío / to feel (to be) cold (persons)
tener ganas de + infinitive / to feel like + present participle

> *Tengo ganas de tomar un helado.* / I feel like having an ice cream.

tener gusto en + infinitive / to be glad + infinitive

> *Tengo mucho gusto en conocerle.* / I am very glad to meet you.

tener hambre / to feel (to be) hungry
tener la bondad de / please; please be good enough to . . .

> *Tenga la bondad de cerrar la puerta.* / Please close the door.

tener la culpa de algo / to take the blame for something, to be
  to blame for something

> *Tengo la culpa de eso.* / I am to blame for that.

tener lugar / to take place

> *El accidente tuvo lugar anoche.* / The accident took place last
>   night.

tener miedo de / to be afraid of
tener mucha sed / to feel (to be) very thirsty (persons)
tener mucho calor / to feel (to be) very warm (persons)
tener mucho frío / to feel (to be) very cold (persons)
tener mucho que hacer / to have a lot to do
tener poco que hacer / to have little to do
tener prisa / to be in a hurry
tener que + infinitive / to have + infinitive

> *Tengo que estudiar.* / I have to study.

tener razón / to be right

> *Ud. tiene razón.* / You are right.

no tener razón / to be wrong

> *Ud. no tiene razón.* / You are wrong.

tener sed / to feel (to be) thirsty (persons)
tener sueño / to feel (to be) sleepy
tener suerte / to be lucky

---

with *todo, toda, todos, todas*

---

a todo / at most
a todo correr / at full speed
ante todo / first of all, in the first place
así y todo / in spite of everything
de todos modos / anyway, in any case, at any rate
en un todo / in all its parts
en todo y por todo / in each and every way
ir a todo correr / to run by leaps and bounds

por todo / throughout
sobre todo / above all, especially
toda la familia / the whole family
todas las noches / every night
todas las semanas / every week
todo el mundo / everybody
todos cuantos / all those that
todos los años / every year
todos los días / every day

with *vez* and *veces*

a la vez / at the same time
a veces / sometimes, at times
alguna vez / sometime
algunas veces / sometimes
cada vez / each time
cada vez más / more and more (each time)
de vez en cuando / from time to time
dos veces / twice, two times
en vez de / instead of
muchas veces / many times
otra vez / again, another time, once more
raras veces / few times, rarely
tal vez / perhaps
una vez / once, one time
una vez más / once more, one more time
unas veces / sometimes
varias veces / several times

with *y*

dicho y hecho / no sooner said than done
sano y salvo / safe and sound

un billete de ida y vuelta / a round-trip ticket
¿Y bien? / And then? And so? So what?
y eso que / even though
y por si eso fuera poco . . . / and as if that were not
  enough . . .

---

with *ya*

¡Hazlo ya! ¡Hágalo ya! / Do it now!
no ya . . . sino / not only . . . but also
¡Pues ya! / Of course! Certainly!
si ya . . . / if only . . .
¡Ya lo creo! / I should certainly think so! Of course!
Ya lo veré. / I'll see to it.
ya no / no longer
Ya pasó. / It's all over now.
ya que / since, as long as, seeing that . . .
¡Ya se ve! / Yes, indeed!
¡Ya voy! / I'm coming! I'll be there in a second!

§13.
Dates, Days, Months, Seasons

§13.1 DATES

> *¿Cuál es la fecha?* / What's the date?
> *¿Cuál es la fecha de hoy?* / What's the date today?
> *Es el primero de junio.* / It is June first.
> *Es el dos de mayo.* / It is May second.

Note that when stating the date, in Spanish we use *el primero*, which is an ordinal number, for the first day of any month. To state all other dates, use the cardinal numbers: *Hoy es el dos de enero, el tres de febrero, el cuatro de marzo,* etc.

> *¿A cuántos estamos hoy?* / What's the date today?
> *Estamos a cinco de abril.* / It's April 5th.

When stating a date, the English word "on" is expressed in Spanish by using the definite article *el* in front of the date:

> *María nació el cuatro de julio.* / Mary was born on the fourth of July.

- When stating the year, in Spanish we use thousand and hundreds:

  > *el año mil novecientos noventa y nueve* / the year 1999

This is very different from English, which is usually stated as nineteen ninety or nineteen hundred ninety. In Spanish we must state *mil* (one thousand) + *novecientos* (nine hundred): *mil novecientos noventa y nueve* (1999).

- To sum up: *Hoy es jueves, el veintidós de noviembre, de dos mil doce.* / Today is Thursday, November 22, 2012.
- Note also: *dos mil uno* (2001), *dos mil diez* (2010), and so on.

§13.2 DAYS

- The days of the week, which are all masculine, are:

domingo / Sunday; *lunes* / Monday; *martes* / Tuesday; *miércoles* / Wednesday; *jueves* / Thursday; *viernes* / Friday; *sábado* / Saturday.

- In Spanish, the days of the week are ordinarily not capitalized. In newspapers, magazines, business letters, and elsewhere, you sometimes see them capitalized.
- When stating the day of the week in English we may use "on," but in Spanish we use *el* or *los* in front of the day of the week.

    el lunes / on Monday; *los lunes* / on Mondays

Note that the days of the week whose last letter is *s* do not change in the plural: *el martes / los martes; el miércoles / los miércoles.* BUT: *el sábado / los sábados; el domingo / los domingos.*

    ¿Qué día es? / What day is it?
    ¿Qué día es hoy? / What day is it today?
    Hoy es lunes. / Today is Monday.

§13.3 MONTHS

- The months of the year, which are all masculine, are:

enero / January; *febrero* / February; *marzo* / March; *abril* / April; *mayo* / May; *junio* / June; *julio* / July; *agosto* / August; *septiembre* / September; *octubre* / October; *noviembre* / November; *diciembre* / December.

- In Spanish, the months of the year are ordinarily not capitalized. In newspapers, magazines, business letters, and elsewhere, you sometimes see them capitalized.
- To say in + the name of the month, use en: *en enero* / in January; OR: *en el mes de enero* / in the month of January.
- The plural of *el mes* is *los meses*.

§13.4 SEASONS

- The seasons of the year *(las estaciones del año)* are:

> *la primavera* / spring; *el verano* / summer; *el otoño* / autumn, fall; *el invierno* / winter.

- In Spanish, the seasons of the year are not capitalized.
- The definite article usually precedes a season of the year:

> *¿En qué estación hace frío?* / In what season is it cold?
> *Generalmente, hace frío en el invierno.* / Generally, it is cold in winter.

§14.

Telling Time

§14.1 TIME EXPRESSIONS YOU OUGHT TO KNOW

¿Qué hora es? / What time is it?
Es la una. / It is one o'clock.

Note that the 3rd person singular of *ser* is used because the time is one (o'clock), which is singular.

Son las dos. / It is two o'clock.

Note that the 3rd person plural of *ser* is used because the time is two (o'clock), which is more than one.

Son las tres; son las cuatro. / It is three o'clock; it is four o'clock.

When the time is a certain number of minutes after the hour, the hour is stated first *(Es la una)* + *y* + the number of minutes:

Es la una y cinco. / It is five minutes after one o'clock (It is 1:05).
Son las dos y diez. / It is ten minutes after two o'clock
(It is 2:10).

When the hour is a quarter after, you can express it by using either *y cuarto* or *y quince (minutos)*:

Son las dos y cuarto OR *Son las dos y quince (minutos).* / It is
2:15.

When it is half past the hour, you can express it by using either *y media* or *y treinta (minutos)*:

Son las dos y media OR *Son las dos y treinta.* / It is 2:30.

When the time is a certain number of minutes of (to, toward, before) the hour, state the hour that it will be + *menos* + the number of minutes. If it is 15 minutes before the hour, use *menos cuarto* (a quarter of).

Son las cinco menos veinte. / It is twenty minutes to five OR It is 4:40.

Son las cuatro menos cuarto. / It is a quarter of (to) four OR It is 3:45.

When you are not telling what time it is and you want only to say at a certain time, merely say:

a la una, a las dos, a las tres / at one o'clock, at two o'clock, at three o'clock

a la una y cuarto / at 1:15; *a las cuatro y media* / at 4:30

¿A qué hora va Ud. a la clase de español? / At what time do you go to Spanish class?

Voy a la clase a las dos y veinte. / I go to class at 2:20.

¿A qué hora toma Ud. el almuerzo? / At what time do you have lunch?

Tomo el almuerzo a las doce en punto. / I have lunch at exactly twelve o'clock.

¿A qué hora toma Ud. el autobús para ir a la escuela? / At what time do you take the bus to go to school?

Tomo el autobús a las ocho en punto. / I take the bus at eight o'clock sharp.

¿Llega Ud. a la escuela a tiempo? / Do you arrive at school on time?

Llego a la escuela a eso de las ocho y media. / I arrive at school at about 8:30.

When you state what time it is or at what time you are going to do something, sometimes you have to make it clear whether it is in the morning (A.M.), in the afternoon (P.M.), or in the evening (P.M.):

Tomo el tren a las ocho de la noche. / I am taking the train at 8:00 P.M. (at eight o'clock in the evening).

Tomo el tren a las ocho de la mañana. / I am taking the train at 8:00 A.M. (at eight o'clock in the morning).

Tomo el tren a las cuatro de la tarde. / I am taking the train at 4:00 P.M. (at four o'clock in the afternoon).

Tomo el tren a las tres de la madrugada. / I am taking the train at 3:00 A.M. (at three o'clock in the morning).

Note that in Spanish we say *de la madrugada* (before daylight hours) instead of *de la noche* if the time is between midnight and the break of dawn.

¿Qué hora es? / What time is it? *Es mediodía.* / It is noon.
¿Qué hora es? / What time is it? *Es medianoche.* / It is
  midnight.
¿A qué hora toma Ud. el almuerzo? / At what time do you
  have lunch?
Tomo el almuerzo a mediodía (OR *al mediodía*). / I have
  lunch at noon.
¿A qué hora se acuesta Ud. por lo general? / At what time
  do you generally get to bed?
Generalmente, me acuesto a medianoche (or *a la
  medianoche*). / Generally, I go to bed at midnight.

When telling time in the past, use the imperfect indicative
tense of the verb *ser:*

Eran las dos cuando tomé el almuerzo hoy. / It was two
  o'clock when I had lunch today.
Era la una cuando los vi. / It was one o'clock when I saw
  them.
¿Qué hora era cuando sus padres llegaron a casa? / What
  time was it when your parents arrived home?
Eran las dos de la madrugada. / It was two in the morning.

The future tense is used when telling time in the future or
when you wonder what time it is at present or when you want
to state what time it probably is:

En algunos minutos serán las tres. / In a few minutes it will
  be three o'clock.
¿Qué hora será? / I wonder what time it is.
Serán las seis. / It is probably six o'clock.

When wondering what time it was in the past or when stating what time it probably was in the past, use the conditional:

> *¿Qué hora sería?* / I wonder what time it was. *Serían las seis cuando llegaron.* / It was probably six o'clock when they arrived.

When no specific time is stated and you merely want to say in the morning, in the afternoon, or in the evening, use the preposition *por* instead of *de*:

> *Los sábados estudio mis lecciones por la mañana, juego por la tarde, y salgo por la noche.* / On Saturdays I study my lessons in the morning, I play in the afternoon, and I go out in the evening.

To express a little after the hour, state the hour + *y pico*:

> *Cuando salí eran las seis y pico.* / When I went out it was a little after six o'clock.

To say about or around a particular time, say *a eso de* + the hour:

> *Te veré a eso de la una.* / I will see you about one o'clock.
> *Te veré a eso de las tres.* / I will see you around three o'clock.

Instead of using *menos* (of, to, toward, before the hour), you may use the verb *faltar*, which means "to be lacking": *Faltan cinco minutos para las tres.* / It's five minutes to three (in other words, five minutes are lacking before it is three o'clock). In this construction, which is idiomatic, note the use of the preposition *para.*

§14.2 "OFFICIAL" TIME EXPRESSIONS

Finally, note another way to tell time, which is used on radio and TV, in railroad and bus stations, at airports, and at other places where many people gather. It is the 24-hour system around the clock.

When using the 24 hours around the clock, the stated time is perfectly clear and there is no need to say *de la madrugada, de la mañana, de la tarde,* or *de la noche.*

When using the 24-hour system, there is no need to use *cuarto, media, menos,* or *y* (except when *y* is required in the cardinal number: *diez y seis*).

When you hear or see the stated time using this system, subtract 12 from the number that you hear or see. If the number is less than 12, it is A.M. time. Midnight is *veinticuatro horas.* This system uses the cardinal numbers. Note that a decimal point is used in Spanish when we would use a colon in English, as shown below.

---

trece horas / 1 P.M. (13 – 12 = 1)
catorce horas / 2 P.M. (14 – 12 = 2)
veinte horas / 8 P.M. (20 – 12 = 8)
quince horas treinta / 15.30, 3:30 P.M. (15 – 12 = 3)
veinte horas cuarenta y dos / 20.42, 8:42 P.M. (20 – 12 = 8)
nueve horas diez / 09.10, 9:10 A.M.

§15.
Weather Expressions

¿Qué tiempo hace? / What is the weather like?

Hace buen tiempo. / The weather is good.

Hace calor. / It is warm (hot).

Hace fresco hoy. / It is cool today.

Hace frío. / It is cold.

Hace mal tiempo. / The weather is bad.

Hace sol. / It is sunny.

Hace viento. / It is windy.

¿Qué tiempo hacía cuando Ud. salió esta mañana? / What was the weather like when you went out this morning?

Hacía mucho frío ayer por la noche. / It was very cold yesterday evening.

Hacía mucho viento. / It was very windy.

¿Qué tiempo hará mañana? / What will the weather be like tomorrow?

Se dice que hará mucho calor. / They say it will be very hot.

Hay lodo. / It is muddy. *Había lodo.* / It was muddy.

Hay luna. / The moon is shining. OR There is moonlight.

Había luna ayer por la noche. / There was moonlight yesterday evening.

¿Hay mucha nieve aquí en el invierno? / Is there much snow here in winter?

Hay neblina. / It is foggy. *Había mucha neblina.* / It was very foggy.

Hay polvo. / It is dusty. *Había mucho polvo.* / It was very dusty.

Other weather expressions

Está lloviendo ahora. / It is raining now.

Está nevando. / It is snowing.

Esta mañana llovía cuando tomé el autobús. / This morning it
  was raining when I took the bus.

Estaba lloviendo cuando tomé el autobús. / It was raining
  when I took the bus.

Estaba nevando cuando me desperté. / It was snowing when I
  woke up.

¿Nieva mucho aquí en el invierno? / Does it snow much here
  in winter?

Las estrellas brillan. / The stars are shining.

¿Le gusta a usted la lluvia? / Do you like rain?

¿Le gusta a usted la nieve? / Do you like snow?

§16.
Numbers

§16.1 CARDINAL NUMBERS: ZERO TO ONE HUNDRED MILLION

0 *cero*	27 *veintisiete*
1 *uno, una*	28 *veintiocho*
2 *dos*	29 *veintinueve*
3 *tres*	30 *treinta*
4 *cuatro*	31 *treinta y uno, treinta y una*
5 *cinco*	
6 *seis*	32 *treinta y dos*, etc.
7 *siete*	
8 *ocho*	40 *cuarenta*
9 *nueve*	41 *cuarenta y uno, cuarenta y una*
10 *diez*	
11 *once*	42 *cuarenta y dos*, etc.
12 *doce*	
13 *trece*	50 *cincuenta*
14 *catorce*	51 *cincuenta y uno, cinuenta y una*
15 *quince*	
16 *dieciséis*	52 *cincuenta y dos*, etc.
17 *diecisiete*	
18 *dieciocho*	60 *sesenta*
19 *diecinueve*	61 *sesenta y uno, sesenta y una*
20 *veinte*	
21 *veintiuno*	62 *sesenta y dos*, etc.
22 *veintidós*	
23 *veintitrés*	70 *setenta*
24 *veinticuatro*	71 *setenta y uno, setenta y una*
25 *veinticinco*	
26 *veintiséis*	72 *setenta y dos*, etc.

80	*ochenta*	1,000	*mil*
81	*ochenta y uno,*	2,000	*dos mil*
	ochenta y una	3,000	*tres mil*, etc.
82	*ochenta y dos,*		
	etc.	100,000	*cien mil*
		200,000	*doscientos mil,*
90	*noventa*		*doscientas mil*
91	*noventa y uno,*	300,000	*trescientos mil,*
	noventa y una		*trescientas mil,*
92	*noventa y dos*, etc.		etc.
100	*ciento (cien)*	1,000,000	*un millón (de +*
101	*ciento uno,*		noun)
	ciento una	2,000,000	*dos millones (de*
102	*ciento dos*, etc.		*+ noun)*
		3,000,000	*tres millones (de*
200	*doscientos,*		*+ noun)*
	doscientas		
300	*trescientos,*	100,000,000	*cien millones*
	trescientas		*(de + noun)*
400	*cuatrocientos,*		
	cuatrocientas		**Approximate**
500	*quinientos,*		**numbers**
	quinientas		*unos veinte*
600	*seiscientos,*		*libros* / about
	seiscientas		(some) twenty
700	*setecientos,*		books
	setecientas		*unas treinta*
800	*ochocientos,*		*personas* / about
	ochocientas		(some) thirty
900	*novecientos,*		persons
	novecientas		

Simple arithmetical expressions

dos y dos son cuatro	$2 + 2 = 4$
diez menos cinco son cinco	$10 - 5 = 5$
tres por cinco son quince	$3 \times 5 = 15$
diez dividido por dos son cinco	$10 \div 2 = 5$

---

§16.2 ORDINAL NUMBERS: FIRST TO TENTH

---

primero, primer, primera	first	1st
segundo, segunda	second	2nd
tercero, tercer, tercera	third	3rd
cuarto, cuarta	fourth	4th
quinto, quinta	fifth	5th
sexto, sexta	sixth	6th
séptimo, séptima	seventh	7th
octavo, octava	eighth	8th
noveno, novena	ninth	9th
décimo, décima	tenth	10th

Note that beyond 10th the cardinal numbers are used instead of the ordinal numbers, but when there is a noun involved, the cardinal number is placed after the noun:

el día 15, el día quince / the fifteenth day

Note also that in titles of monarchs, etc., the definite article is not used between the person's name and the number, as it is in English:

Alfonso XIII, Alfonso Trece / Alfonso the Thirteenth

And note that *noveno* changes to *nono* in such titles:

Luis IX, Luis Nono / Louis the Ninth

§17.

Synonyms

There are many Spanish words that are approximate in meaning to another. A list of these synonyms follows, along with the English counterparts.

acercarse (a), aproximarse (a) / to approach, to come near
acordarse (de), recordar / to remember
alabar, elogiar / to praise, to glorify, to eulogize
alimento, comida / food, nourishment
alumno (alumna), estudiante / pupil, student
andar, caminar / to walk
anillo, sortija / ring (finger)
antiguo (antigua), viejo (vieja) / ancient, old
asustar, espantar / to frighten, to terrify, to scare
atreverse (a), osar / to dare, to venture
aún, todavía / still, yet, even
ayuda, socorro, auxilio / aid, succor, help, assistance
barco, buque, vapor / boat, ship
bastante, suficiente / enough, sufficient
batalla, combate, lucha / battle, combat, struggle, fight
bonito (bonita), lindo (linda) / pretty
breve, corto (corta) / brief, short
burlarse de, mofarse de / to make fun of, to mock
camarero (camarera), mozo (moza) / server
campesino (campesina), rústico (rústica), labrador (labradora) / farmer, peasant
cara, rostro, semblante / face
cariño, amor / affection, love
cocinar, cocer, guisar / to cook
comenzar, empezar, principiar / to begin, to start, to commence
comprender, entender / to understand, to comprehend
conquistar, vencer / to conquer, to vanquish

185

contento (contenta), feliz, alegre / content, happy, glad
contestar, responder / to answer, to reply
continuar, seguir / to continue
cruzar, atravesar / to cross
cuarto, habitación / room
cura, sacerdote / priest
chiste, chanza, broma / jest, joke, fun
dar un paseo, pasearse / to take a walk, to go for a walk
dar voces, gritar / to shout, to cry out
delgado (delgada), esbelto (esbelta), flaco (flaca) / thin,
    slender, slim, svelte
desafortunado, desgraciado / unfortunate
desaparecer, desvanecerse / to disappear, to vanish
desear, querer / to desire, to want, to wish
desprecio, desdén / scorn, disdain, contempt
diablo, demonio / devil, demon
diferente, distinto (distinta) / different, distinct
diversión, pasatiempo / diversion, pastime
echar, lanzar, tirar, arrojar / to throw, to lance, to hurl
elevar, levantar, alzar / to elevate, to raise, to lift
empleado (empleada), dependiente / employee, clerk
enojarse, enfadarse / to become angry, to become annoyed
enviar, mandar / to send
error, falta / error, mistake, fault
escoger, elegir / to choose, to select, to elect
esperar, aguardar / to wait for
esposa, mujer / wife, spouse
estrecho (estrecha), angosto (angosta) / narrow
famoso (famosa), célebre, ilustre / famous, celebrated,
    renowned, illustrious
fiebre, calentura / fever
grave, serio (seria) / serious, grave
habilidad, destreza / ability, skill, dexterity
hablador (habladora), locuaz / talkative, loquacious
halagar, adular / to flatter
hallar, encontrar / to find
hermoso (hermosa), bello (bella) / beautiful, handsome

igual, semejante / equal, alike, similar
invitar, convidar / to invite
irse, marcharse / to leave, to go away
joya, alhaja / jewel, gem
lanzar, tirar, echar / to throw, to lance, to hurl
lengua, idioma / language, idiom
lentamente, despacio / slowly
luchar, combatir, pelear, pugnar / to fight, to battle, to combat, to struggle
lugar, sitio / place, site
llevar, conducir / to take, to lead
maestro (maestra), profesor (profesora) / teacher, professor
marido, esposo / husband, spouse
miedo, temor / fear, dread
morir, fallecer / to die, to expire
mostrar, enseñar / to show
nobleza, hidalguez, hidalguía / nobility
nunca, jamás / never
obtener, conseguir / to obtain, to get
odiar, aborrecer / to hate, to abhor
onda, ola / wave
país, nación / country, nation
pájaro, ave / bird
pararse, detenerse / to stop (oneself)
parecido, semejante / like, similar
pasar un buen rato, divertirse / to have a good time
pena, dolor / pain, grief
perezoso (perezosa), flojo (floja) / lazy
periódico, diario / newspaper
permiso, licencia / permission, leave
permitir, dejar / to permit, to allow, to let
poner, colocar / to put, to place
posponer, diferir, aplazar / to postpone, to defer, to put off, to delay
premio, galardón / prize, reward
quedarse, permanecer / to remain, to stay
rapidez, prisa, velocidad / rapidly, haste, speed, velocity

regresar, volver / to return (to a place)
rezar, orar / to pray
rogar, suplicar / to beg, to implore, to entreat
romper, quebrar / to break
sin embargo, no obstante / nevertheless, however
solamente, sólo / only
sorprender, asombrar / to surprise, to astonish
suceso, acontecimiento / happening, event
sufrir, padecer / to suffer, to endure
susto, espanto / fright, scare, dread
tal vez, acaso, quizá, quizás / maybe, perhaps
terminar, acabar, concluir / to terminate, to finish, to end
tonto (tonta), necio (necia) / foolish, stupid, idiotic
trabajo, tarea, obra / work, task
tratar de, intentar / to try to, to attempt
ya que, puesto que / since, inasmuch as

Tip	To increase your Spanish vocabulary, play the following word game.

When you see a license plate on a vehicle, take a good look at the letters. There are usually two or three.

See how many Spanish words you can think of that contain those letters. They can be in the same order or in any order in the word that you recall. The words can be nouns, pronouns, adjectives, adverbs, conjugated verbs, or infinitives.

Examples:
JAO   You write, for example, *bajo* (low, below), *trabajo* (work, I work), *ajo* (garlic).
NIS   You write, for example, *sin* (without), *insecto* (insect).

If you get stuck, use the vocabulary in this book or in a Spanish-English dictionary. It's a fun way to flip through the pages of a dictionary. Just don't play this game while you're driving!

§18.

Antonyms

Antonyms are words with opposite meanings. Here is a list of antonyms in Spanish, with the English translation of each word.

aburrirse / to be bored; *divertirse* / to have a good time
aceptar / to accept; *ofrecer* / to offer
acordarse de / to remember; *olvidar, olvidarse de* / to forget
admitir / to admit; *negar* / to deny
agradecido, agradecida / thankful; *ingrato, ingrata* / thankless
alejarse de / to go away from; *acercarse a* / to approach
algo / something; *nada* / nothing
alguien / someone; *nadie* / no one
alguno (algún) / some; *ninguno (ningún)* / none
amar / to love; *odiar* / to hate
amigo, amiga / friend; *enemigo, enemiga* / enemy
ancho, ancha / wide; *estrecho, estrecha* / narrow
antes (de) / before; *después (de)* / after
antiguo, antigua / ancient, old; *moderno, moderna* / modern
antipático, antipática / unpleasant; *simpático, simpática* / nice
   (people)
aparecer / to appear; *desaparecer* / to disappear
aplicado, aplicada / industrious; *flojo, floja* / lazy
apresurarse a / to hasten, to hurry; *tardar en* / to delay
aprisa / quickly; *despacio* / slowly
aquí / here; *allí* / there
arriba / above, upstairs; *abajo* / below, downstairs
ausente / absent; *presente* / present
bajar / to go down; *subir* / to go up
bajo, baja / low, short; *alto, alta* / high, tall
bien / well; *mal* / badly, poorly
bueno (buen), buena / good; *malo (mal), mala* / bad
caballero / gentleman; *dama* / lady

caliente / hot; *frío, fría* / cold

caro, cara / expensive; *barato, barata* / cheap

cerca (de) / near; *lejos (de)* / far

cerrar / to close; *abrir* / to open

claro, clara / light; *oscuro, oscura* / dark

cobarde / cowardly; *valiente* / valiant, brave

cómico, cómica / comic, funny; *trágico, trágica* / tragic

comprar / to buy; *vender* / to sell

común / common; *raro, rara* / rare

con / with; *sin* / without

contra / against; *con* / with

corto, corta / short; *largo, larga* / long

costoso, costosa / costly, expensive; *barato, barata* / cheap, inexpensive

culpable / guilty, culpable; *inocente* / innocent

dar / to give; *recibir* / to receive

débil / weak, debilitated; *fuerte* / strong

dejar caer / to drop; *recoger* / to pick up

delante de / in front of; *detrás de* / in back of

delgado, delgada / thin; *gordo, gorda* / stout, fat

dentro / inside; *fuera* / outside

derrota / defeat; *victoria* / victory

descansar / to rest; *cansar* / to tire; *cansarse* / to get tired

descubrir / to uncover; *cubrir* / to cover

descuido / carelessness; *esmero* / meticulousness

desgraciado, desgraciada / unfortunate; *afortunado, afortunada* / fortunate

despertarse / to wake up; *dormirse* / to fall asleep

destruir / to destroy; *crear* / to create

desvanecerse / to disappear; *aparecer* / to appear

distinto, distinta / different; *semejante* / similar

dulce / sweet; *amargo* / bitter

duro, dura / hard; *suave, blando, blanda* / soft

elogiar / to praise; *censurar* / to criticize

empezar / to begin, to start; *terminar, acabar* / to end

encender / to light; *apagar* / to extinguish

encima (de) / on top; *debajo (de)* / under

entrada / entrance; *salida* / exit

esta noche / tonight, this evening; *anoche* / last night, yesterday evening

este / east; *oeste* / west

estúpido, estúpida / stupid; *inteligente* / intelligent

éxito / success; *fracaso* / failure

fácil / easy; *difícil* / difficult

fatigado, fatigada / tired; *descansado, descansada* / rested

feliz / happy; *triste* / sad

feo, fea / ugly; *hermoso, hermosa* / beautiful; *bello, bella* / beautiful

fin / end; *principio* / beginning

flaco, flaca / thin; *gordo, gorda* / fat

gastar / to spend (money); *ahorrar* / to save (money)

gigante / giant; *enano, enana* / dwarf

grande (gran) / large, big; *pequeño, pequeña* / small, little

guerra / war; *paz* / peace

hablador, habladora / talkative; *taciturno, taciturna* / silent, taciturn

hablar / to talk, to speak; *callarse* / to keep silent

hembra / female; *macho* / male

ida / departure; *vuelta* / return (*ida y vuelta* / round trip)

ignorar / not to know; *saber* / to know

interesante / interesting; *aburrido, aburrida* / boring

inútil / useless; *útil* / useful

ir / to go; *venir* / to come

joven / young; *viejo, vieja* / old

jugar / to play; *trabajar* / to work

juventud / youth; *vejez* / old age

lejano / distant; *cercano* / nearby

lentitud / slowness; *rapidez* / speed

levantarse / to get up; *sentarse* / to sit down

libertad / liberty; *esclavitud* / slavery

limpio, limpia / clean; *sucio, sucia* / dirty

luz / light; *sombra* / shadow

llegada / arrival; *partida* / departure

llenar / to fill; *vaciar* / to empty

lleno, llena / full; *vacío, vacía* / empty

llorar / to cry, to weep; *reír* / to laugh

maldecir / to curse; *bendecir* / to bless

mañana / tomorrow; *ayer* / yesterday

más / more; *menos* / less

mejor / better; *peor* / worse

menor / younger; *mayor* / older

mentir / to lie; *decir la verdad* / to tell the truth

mentira / lie, falsehood; *verdad* / truth

meter / to put in; *sacar* / to take out

mismo, misma / same; *diferente* / different

mucho, mucha / much; *poco, poca* / little

nacer / to be born; *morir* / to die

natural / natural; *innatural* / unnatural

necesario / necessary; *innecesario* / unnecessary

negar / to deny; *otorgar* / to grant

noche / night; *día* / day

obeso, obesa / obese, fat; *delgado, delgada* / thin

obscuro, obscura / dark; *claro, clara* / light

odio / hate, hatred; *amor* / love

orgulloso, orgullosa / proud; *humilde* / humble

oriental / eastern; *occidental* / western

peligro / danger; *seguridad* / safety

perder / to lose; *ganar* / to win; *hallar* / to find

perezoso, perezosa / lazy; *diligente* / diligent

permitir / to permit; *prohibir* / to prohibit

pesado, pesada / heavy; *ligero, ligera* / light

ponerse / to put on (clothing); *quitarse* / to take off (clothing)

porvenir / future; *pasado* / past

posible / possible; *imposible* / impossible

pregunta / question; *respuesta, contestación* / answer

preguntar / to ask; *contestar* / to answer

presente / present; *ausente* / absent

prestar / to lend; *pedir prestado* / to borrow

primero (primer), primera / first; *último, última* / last
puesta del sol / sunset; *salida del sol* / sunrise
quedarse / to remain; *irse* / to leave, to go away
quizá(s) / maybe, perhaps; *seguro, cierto* / sure, certain
recto / straight; *tortuoso* / winding
rico, rica / rich; *pobre* / poor
riqueza / wealth; *pobreza* / poverty
rubio, rubia / blond; *moreno, morena* / brunette
ruido / noise; *silencio* / silence
sabio, sabia / wise; *tonto, tonta* / foolish
salir (de) / to leave (from); *entrar (en)* / to enter (in, into)
seco / dry; *mojado* / wet
separar / to separate; *juntar* / to join
sí / yes; *no* / no
siempre / always; *nunca* / never
subir / to go up; *bajar* / to go down
sucio / dirty; *limpio* / clean
sur / south; *norte* / north
temprano / early; *tarde* / late
tomar / to take; *dar* / to give
tonto / foolish; *listo* / clever
tranquilo / tranquil, peaceful; *turbulento* / restless, turbulent
unir / to unite; *desunir* / to disunite
usual / usual; *extraño, raro* / unusual
vida / life; *muerte* / death
virtud / virtue; *vicio* / vice
y / and, plus; *menos* / minus, less

§19.

Cognates

Another good way to increase your vocabulary is to become aware of cognates. A cognate is a word whose origin is the same as another word in other languages. There are many cognates in Spanish and English. Their spelling is sometimes identical or very similar in both languages. Most of the time, the meaning is the same or similar; sometimes they appear to be related because of the similar or identical spelling but they are not true cognates. Those are described as "false cognates" – for example, the Spanish word *actual* means present-day, not actual; the English word actual is expressed in Spanish as *real*, *verdadero*, *efectivo*, or *existente*. Also, the Spanish word *pan* means bread, not pan. The English word pan is *cacerola*, *cazuela*, or *sartén* in Spanish.

Generally speaking, Spanish words that have certain endings have equivalent endings in English.

Spanish Ending of a Word	Equivalent English Ending of a Word
-ario	-ary
-ción	-tion
-dad	-ty
-fía	-phy
-ia	-y
-ía	-y
-io	-y
-ista	-ist
-mente	-ly
-orio	-ory
-oso	-ous

Tip

Also note that Spanish words that begin with *es* are generally equivalent to an English word that begins with s. Just drop the *e* in the beginning of the Spanish word and you have a close equivalent to the spelling of an English word.

especial / special; *estudiante* / student

Here are examples to illustrate **true cognates** whose spellings are identical or similar:

actor / actor	*historia* / history
admiración / admiration	*hotel* / hotel
atención / attention	*idea* / idea
autoridad / authority	*invitación* / invitation
central / central	*manual* / manual
civilización / civilization	*nación* / nation
color / color	*naturalmente* / naturally
correctamente / correctly	*necesario* / necessary
chocolate / chocolate	*necesidad* / necessity
dentista / dentist	*novelista* / novelist
doctor / doctor	*piano* / piano
dormitorio / dormitory, bedroom	*posibilidad* / possibility
escena / scene	*radio* / radio
estúpido / stupid	*realidad* / reality
famoso / famous	*remedio* / remedy
farmacia / pharmacy	*sección* / section
finalmente / finally	*sociedad* / society
fotografía / photography	*universidad* / university
generoso / generous	*violín* / violin
geografía / geography	*vocabulario* / vocabulary

§20.
Tricky Words

Some Spanish words resemble English words, but their meanings are not what you would expect.

actual / present, of the present time, of the present day
antiguo, antigua / former, old, ancient
la apología / eulogy, defense
la arena / sand
asistir a / to attend, to be present at
atender / to attend to, to take care of
la bala / bullet, shot, bale, ball
bizarro, bizarra / brave, gallant, generous
el campo / field, country(side), military camp
el cargo / duty, post, responsibility, burden, load
el collar / necklace
colorado, colorada / red, ruddy
la complexión / temperament, constitution
la conferencia / lecture
la confianza / confidence, trust
la confidencia / secret, trust
constipado, constipada / having a head cold or common cold
la consulta / conference
convenir / to agree, to fit, to suit, to be suitable
la chanza / joke, fun
de / from, of
dé / give
la decepción / disappointment
la desgracia / misfortune
el desmayo / fainting
diario, diaria / daily
el diario / diary, journal, daily newspaper
disfrutar / to enjoy
divisar / to perceive indistinctly
el dormitorio / bedroom, dormitory
el editor / publisher
embarazada / pregnant
emocionante / touching (causing an emotion)

esperar / to hope, to expect, to wait for
el éxito / success, outcome
la fábrica / factory
hay / there is, there are (idiomatic)
el idioma / language
ignorar / not to know, to be unaware
intoxicar / to poison, to intoxicate
el labrador / farmer
largo, larga / long
la lectura / reading
la librería / bookstore
la maleta / valise, suitcase
el mantel / tablecloth
mayor / greater, older
la mesura / moderation
el palo / stick, pole
el pan / bread
pasar / to happen, to pass
el pastel / pie; *la pintura al pastel* / pastel painting
pinchar / to puncture, to prick, to pierce
realizar / to achieve (to realize, in the sense of achieving)
recordar / to remember
el resfriado / common cold (illness)
restar / to deduct, to subtract
sano, sana / healthy
soportar / to tolerate, to bear, to endure, to support
suceder / to happen, to come about, to succeed (follow)
el suceso / event, happening
la tabla / board, plank, table of contents
la tinta / ink, tint
tu / your
tú / you
el vaso / drinking glass

§21.

Proverbs, Sayings, and Common Expressions in Spanish and English

Advice

Anda despacio que tengo prisa. / Make haste slowly. (Easy does it.)

Antes que te cases, mira lo que haces. / Look before you leap. (Literally: Before you get married, look at what you're doing.)

Las paredes tienen oídos. (Las paredes oyen.) / The walls have ears.

Mente sana en cuerpo sano. / A sound mind in a sound body. (From the Latin *mens sana in corpore sano.*)

Poco a poco se anda lejos. / One step at a time. (Literally: Little by little, one goes far away.)

Un lugar / sitio para cada cosa y cada cosa en su lugar / sitio. / A place for everything and everything in its place.

Vale más una imagen que mil palabras. / A picture is worth a thousand words.

Vela que arde por las dos puntas, poco dura. / A candle that burns at both ends lasts only a short time. (Don't burn the candle at both ends.)

Ver es creer. / Seeing is believing.

Animals

Cuando el gato no está, el ratón se pasea. / When the cat's away, the mice will play. (When the cat's away, the mouse takes a walk.)

Cuando el gato va a sus devociones, bailan los ratones. / When the cat's away, the mice will play.

En boca cerrada no entran moscas. / Silence is golden.
(Literally: Flies do not enter a closed mouth.)
Gato que duerme no caza ratónes. / A sleeping cat doesn't
catch mice. (You snooze, you lose.)

Behavior

Cuando (tú) estés en Roma, haz como los romanos. / When in
Rome, do as the Romans do.
El ejercicio hace al maestro. / Practice makes perfect.
Haz lo que (yo) digo y no lo que (yo) hago. / Do as I say, not
as I do.
*Para conocer la calidad de un vino, no es necesario beberse
todo el tonel.* / You don't need to drink the whole cask to
know if the wine is good.
Perro que ladra no muerde. / A barking dog does not bite.
(His bark is worse than his bite.)

Encouragement

Donde una puerta se cierra, otra se abre. / When one door
closes, another one opens.
Más vale tarde que nunca. / Better late than never.
Querer es poder. / Where there's a will, there's a way.

Food

Comer para vivir y no vivir para comer. / One should eat to live
and not live to eat.
Después de comer, ni un sobre escrito leer. / After eating,
don't even read an envelope.
Dime qué comes y te diré quien eres. / Tell me what you eat,
and I'll tell you who you are.
No sólo de pan vivirá el hombre. / Man does not live by bread
alone.

Fortune

Bien está lo que bien acaba. / All's well that ends well.

Lo que mal comienza, mal acaba. / What starts badly ends badly.

Friendship

En el peligro, se conoce al amigo. / A friend in need is a friend indeed.

Dime con quién andas y te diré quién eres. / Tell me who your friends are, and I'll tell you who you are.

La amistad no se compra. / Friendship cannot be bought. (Friendship has no price.)

Al decir las verdades se pierdan las amistades. / Friendships are lost when the truth is told.

Aquellos son ricos, que tienen amigos. / Those who have friends are rich.

Money / Power

Él que la hace la paga. / You have to pay the consequences. (You made your bed, now sleep in it.)

El que todo lo quiere, todo lo pierde. / Whoever wants everything loses everything.

El que más tiene más quiere. / The more one has, the more one wants.

La libertad vale más que el oro. / Liberty is worth more than gold.

La unión hace la fuerza. / There is strength in unity.

Más vale pájaro en mano que ciento volando. / A bird in the hand is worth two in the bush. (A bird in the hand is worth a hundred flying in the air.)

Más vale saber que haber. / Knowing is better than having. (Knowledge is worth more than possessions / things.)

No es oro todo lo que reluce / brilla. / All that glitters is not gold.

Paga lo que debes y sabrás lo que tienes. / Pay what you owe and you'll know what you have.

Quien debe y paga no debe nada. / Whoever owes and pays owes nothing.

Saber es poder. / Knowledge is power.

Nature

Después de la tormenta viene la calma. / After the storm comes the calm. (Note that in English we refer to the calm *before* the storm.)

Donde hay humo, hay fuego. / Where there's smoke, there's fire.

No hay rosa sin espina. / Every rose has its thorn. (There is no rose without a thorn.)

Quien siembra vientos recoge tempestades. / If you sow the wind, you will reap the whirlwind.

People

Al decir las verdades se pierdan las amistades. / Friendships are lost when the truth is told.

Aprendiz de todo (mucho), oficial de nada. / Jack of all trades, master of none.

El mal escritor le echa la culpa a la pluma. / The bad writer blames his pen.

El que mal canta, bien le suena. / He who sings badly likes what he hears.

El que mucho duerme poco aprende. / Whoever sleeps a lot learns little.

El que no sabe obedecer no sabe mandar. / Whoever doesn't know how to follow doesn't know how to lead (give orders).

El que no se aventura no cruza el mar. / Nothing ventured, nothing gained. (Whoever doesn't take a risk doesn't cross the sea.)

Quien canta su mal espanta. / When you sing, you drive away your grief.

Religion

A Dios rogando y con el mazo dando. / Put your faith in God and keep your powder dry. (The Lord helps those who help themselves.)

A quien madruga, Dios le ayuda. / The early bird catches the worm. (God helps those who get up early.)

Dios los cría y ellos se juntan. / Birds of a feather flock together.

Speaking

A palabras locas, oídos sordos. / Turn a deaf ear to crazy words.

Antes de hablar es bueno pensar. / (It's good to) think before you speak.

De decir a hacer hay mucho que ver. / There is a great difference between saying and doing.

Quien calla, otorga. / Silence means consent. (*otorgar* to grant, to consent)

Para saber hablar, hay que saber escuchar. / In order to know how to talk, one must know how to listen.

Time

Cada día se aprende algo nuevo. / You learn something new every day.

El tiempo perdido no se recobra. / One can never get back lost time.

Lo que hoy se pierde, se gana mañana. / What is lost today is won tomorrow.

No dejes para mañana lo que puedes hacer hoy. / Don't put off until tomorrow what you can do today.

Definitions of Basic Grammatical Terms with Examples in Spanish and English: Beginner, Intermediate, and Advanced Levels

Active Voice

When we speak or write in the active voice, the subject of the verb performs the action of the verb. The action falls on the direct object if there is one.

Example:
El ladrón abrió la ventana. / The robber opened the window.
　　The subject is *el ladrón*. The verb is *abrió*. The direct object is *la ventana*.

See also **passive voice** in this section. Compare the above sentence with the example in the passive voice.

Adjective

An adjective is a word that modifies a noun or a pronoun. In grammar, to modify a word means to describe, limit, expand, or make the meaning specific.

Examples:
un jardín hermoso / a beautiful garden.
　　The adjective *hermoso* modifies the noun *jardín*.
Ella es bonita. / She is pretty.
　　The adjective *bonita* modifies the pronoun *ella*.

In Spanish there are different kinds of adjectives. See also **comparative adjective**, **demonstrative adjective**, **descriptive adjective**, **interrogative adjective**, **limiting adjective**, **possessive adjective**, and **superlative adjective** in this section. Also consult this book's index.

Adverb

An adverb is a word that modifies a verb, an adjective, or another adverb. An adverb says something about how, when, where, to what extent or in what way.

Examples:
María corre rápidamente. / Mary runs swiftly.

The adverb *rápidamente* modifies the verb *corre*. The adverb shows *how* she runs.

Juan es muy guapo. / John is very handsome.

The adverb *muy* modifies the adjective *guapo*. The adverb shows *how handsome* he is.

El muchacho habla muy rápidamente ahora. / The boy is talking very fast now.

The adverb *muy* modifies the adverb *rápidamente*. The adverb shows *to what extent* he is talking fast. The adverb *ahora* tells us *when*.

La oficina de correos está allá. / The post office is there.

The adverb *allá* modifies the verb *está*. It tells us *where* the post office is.

María escribe meticulosamente. / Mary writes meticulously.

The adverb *meticulosamente* modifies the verb *escribe*. It tells us *in what way* she writes.

Affirmative Statement, Negative Statement

A statement in the affirmative is the opposite of a statement in the negative. When you negate an affirmative statement, you make it negative.

Example in the affirmative:
Me gusta el helado. / I like ice cream.

Example in the negative:
No me gusta el helado. / I do not like ice cream.

Agreement of Adjective with Noun

Agreement is made on the adjective with the noun it modifies in gender (masculine or feminine) and number (singular or plural).

Examples:
una casa blanca / a white house
> The adjective *blanca* is feminine singular because the noun *una casa* is feminine singular.

muchas casas blancas / many white houses
> The adjectives *muchas* and *blancas* are feminine plural because the noun *casas* is feminine plural.

Agreement of Verb with Its Subject

A verb agrees in person (1st, 2nd, or 3rd) and in number (singular or plural) with its subject.

Examples:
Pablo dice la verdad. / Paul tells the truth.
> The verb *dice* (of *decir*) is 3rd person singular because the subject *Pablo* / *Paul* is 3rd person singular.

¿Adónde van los turistas? / Where are the tourists going?
> The verb *van* (of *ir*) is 3rd person plural because the subject *los turistas* / *the tourists* is 3rd person plural.

Antecedent

An antecedent is a word to which a relative pronoun refers. It comes *before* the pronoun.

Examples:
La muchacha que está riendo a carcajadas es mi hermana. / The girl who is laughing loudly is my sister. Note that *está riendo* is the present progressive of *reír*. See §7.5-15.
> The antecedent is *la muchacha*. The relative pronoun *que* refers to the girl.

El coche que yo compré es muy costoso. / The car that I bought is very expensive.
> The antecedent is *el coche*. The relative pronoun *que* refers to the car.

Auxiliary Verb

An auxiliary verb is a helping verb. In English grammar it is *to have*. In Spanish grammar it is *haber*. An auxiliary verb is used to help form the compound tenses.

Example (present perfect tense):
(Yo) he comido. / I <u>have</u> eaten.

Review the six forms of *haber* in the present indicative tense (§7.5-19). You need to know them to form the present perfect tense. You should also review the formation of past participles (§7.3-1). You need to know them to form the seven compound tenses.

Cardinal Number

A cardinal number is a number that expresses an amount, such as *one, two, three,* and so on.

Tip	How many cardinals are sitting on the fence? I see twelve cardinals on the fence.

See also **ordinal number** in this section.

Clause

A clause is a group of words containing a subject and a predicate. A predicate may contain more than one word. A conjugated verb form is revealed in the predicate.

Example:
La señora Gómez vive en un gran apartamento. / Mrs. Gómez lives in a large apartment.
The subject is *la señora Gómez*. The predicate is *vive en un gran apartamento*. The verb is *vive*.

See also **dependent clause**, **independent clause**, and **predicate** in this section.

Comparative Adjective

When making a comparison between two persons or things, an adjective is used to express the degree of comparison in the following ways.

Examples:
Of the same degree of comparison:
Elena es <u>tan alta como</u> María. / Helen is <u>as tall as</u> Mary.

Of a lesser degree of comparison:
Juana es <u>menos inteligente que</u> Eva. / Jane is <u>less intelligent than</u> Eva.

Of a higher degree of comparison:
Esta película <u>es más interesante que</u> ésa. / This movie is <u>more interesting than</u> that one.

See also **superlative adjective** in this section.

Comparative Adverb

An adverb is compared in the same way as an adjective is compared. (See **comparative adjective** above.)

Examples:
Of the same degree of comparison:
El señor Robles habla <u>tan bien como</u> el señor Vega. / Mr. Robles speaks <u>as well as</u> Mr. Vega.

Of a lesser degree of comparison:
Alicia corre <u>menos rápidamente que</u> su hermana. / Alice runs <u>less quickly than</u> her sister.

Of a higher degree of comparison:
Alberto trabaja <u>más lentamente que</u> su hermano. / Albert works <u>more slowly than</u> his brother.

See also **superlative adverb** in this section.

Complex Sentence

A complex sentence contains one independent clause and one or more dependent clauses.

> **Examples:**
> One independent clause and one dependent clause:
> *Carlos toca la guitarra, pero su hermano no toca nada.* / Charles plays the guitar, but his brother doesn't play anything.
>
> The independent clause is *Carlos toca la guitarra*. It makes sense when it stands alone because it expresses a complete thought. The dependent clause is *pero su hermano no toca nada*. The dependent clause, which is introduced by the conjunction *pero*, does not make complete sense when it stands alone because it *depends* on the thought expressed in the independent clause.
>
> One independent clause and two dependent clauses:
> *Ana es una buena alumna porque estudia pero prefiere navegar por internet.* / Anna is a good student because she studies, but she would rather surf the Internet.
>
> The independent clause is *Ana es una buena alumna*. It makes sense when it stands alone because it expresses a complete thought. The first dependent clause is *porque estudia*. This dependent clause, which is introduced by the conjunction *porque*, does not make complete sense when it stands alone because it *depends* on the thought expressed in the independent clause. The second dependent clause is *pero prefiere navegar por internet*. That dependent clause, which is introduced by the conjunction *pero*, does not make complete sense either when it stands alone because it *depends* on the thought expressed in the independent clause.

See also **dependent clause** and **independent clause** in this section.

Compound Sentence

A compound sentence contains two or more independent clauses.

Examples:

La señora Fuentes fue al supermercado, compró algunas cosas, y entonces fue a casa. / Mrs. Fuentes went to the supermarket, she bought a few things, and then she went home.
This compound sentence contains three independent clauses. They are independent because each one makes sense when it stands alone.

Review the explanation, uses, and examples of the **pretérito** in §7.5-3.

Conditional Present Tense

In Spanish grammar, the conditional (el potencial simple) expresses what would happen if a certain condition were met.

Si tuviera bastante dinero, compraría una billetera. / If I had enough money, I would buy a wallet.

It is also used to express conjecture or probability, which is why it is considered a mood in Spanish.

¿Quién estaría a la puerta? / I wonder who was at the door.

See also §7.5-5.

Conjugation

The conjugation of a verb is the fixed order of all its forms showing their inflections (changes) in the three persons of the singular and plural in a particular tense.

Example:

Conjugation of *estudiar* (to study) in the present indicative tense:

estudio	estudiamos
estudias	estudiáis
estudia	estudian

Conjunction

A conjunction is a word that connects words or groups of words.

Examples:

y / and, *o* / or, *pero* / but, *porque* / because

Carlos y Carlota / Charles <u>and</u> Charlotte
(Tú) puedes quedarte en casa o venir conmigo. / You can stay home <u>or</u> you can come with me.

Note that *y* (and) changes to *e* if the word right after it begins with *i* or *hi*.

Examples:

María es bonita e inteligente. / Mary is pretty and intelligent.
Fernando e Isabel / Fernando and Isabel
padre e hijo / father and son; *madre e hija* / mother and daughter

However, if *y* is followed by a word that begins with *hie*, keep *y*: *flores y hierba* / flowers and grass.

Contrary to Fact

This term refers to an "if" clause. See if (*si*) clause in this section.

Declarative Sentence

A declarative sentence makes a statement.

Example:

(Yo) he terminado el trabajo. / I have finished the work.

Definite Article

The definite article in Spanish has four forms and they all mean *the*. They are: *el, la, los,* and *las*.

Examples:
el libro / the book, *la casa* / the house, *los libros* / the books,
las casas / the houses
The definite articles *la*, *los*, and *las* are also used as direct object
pronouns.

See also **direct object pronoun** in this section.

Demonstrative Adjective

A demonstrative adjective is an adjective that points out. It is
placed in front of a noun.

Examples:
este libro / this book; *estos libros* / these books; *esta taza* / this
cup; *estas flores* / these flowers

Demonstrative Pronoun

A demonstrative pronoun is a pronoun that points out. It takes
the place of a noun. It agrees in gender and number with the
noun it replaces.

Examples:
*Tenemos dos teléfonos móviles en venta. ¿Prefiere usted éste o
ése?* / We have two cell phones on sale. Do you prefer this one
or that one?
Prefiero aquéllos. / I prefer those over there.

For demonstrative pronouns that are neuter, see **neuter** in this
section.

Dependent Clause

A dependent clause is a group of words that contains a subject and a predicate. It does not express a complete thought
when it stands alone. It is called *dependent* because it
depends on the independent clause for a complete meaning.
Subordinate clause is another term for dependent clause.

Example:
Eduardo está ausente hoy porque está enfermo. / Edward is absent today because he is sick.
The independent clause is *Eduardo está ausente hoy*. The dependent clause is *porque está enfermo*.

See also **clause** and **independent clause** in this section.

Descriptive Adjective

A descriptive adjective is an adjective that describes a person, place, or thing.

Examples:
una muchacha bonita / a pretty girl; *una casa grande* / a big house; *un carro costoso* / an expensive car

Direct Object Noun

A direct object noun receives the action of the verb *directly*. That is why it is called a direct object, as opposed to an indirect object. A direct object noun is normally placed *after* the verb.

Example:
Escribo un blog. / I am writing a blog.
The direct object is the noun *un blog*.

See also **direct object pronoun** in this section.

Direct Object Pronoun

A direct object pronoun receives the action of the verb *directly*. It takes the place of a direct object noun. In Spanish a pronoun that is a direct object of a verb is ordinarily placed *in front of* the verb.

Example:
La escribo. [the letter = *la carta*] / I am writing it [the letter].

However, in the *affirmative imperative*, a direct object pronoun is placed *after* the verb and is joined to it, resulting in one word.

Example:
¡Escríbala ahora! / Write it [the letter] now!

Note that the accent mark is added on the vowel *i [í]* in order to keep the emphasis on that vowel as it was in *escriba* before the direct object pronoun *la* was added to the verb form. Review the simple rule about stressed vowel sounds in Spanish and when accent marks are needed in §1 and §2.

See also **imperative** in this section.

Disjunctive Pronoun

A disjunctive pronoun is a pronoun that is stressed; in other words, emphasis is placed on it. It is usually the object of a preposition. Prepositional pronoun is another term for disjunctive pronoun.

Examples:
para mí / for me; *para ti* (fam.) / for you; *con usted* / with you;
    con él / with him; *con ella* / with her

Note the following exceptions with *con*:

conmigo / with me; *contigo* (fam.) / with you; *consigo* / with your-
    self (yourselves, himself, herself, themselves).

Ending of a Verb

In Spanish grammar the ending of a verb form changes according to the person and number of the subject and the tense of the verb.

Example:
To form the present indicative tense of a regular *-ar* type verb like *hablar*, drop the *-ar* of the infinitive and add the following endings:

-o, -as, -a for the 1st, 2nd, and 3rd persons of the singular and add *-amos, -áis, -an* for the 1st, 2nd, and 3rd persons of the plural. You then get: *hablo, hablas, habla; hablamos, habláis,* and *hablan.*

See also **stem of a verb**.

Feminine

In Spanish grammar the gender of a noun, pronoun, or adjective is feminine or masculine, not male or female.

Examples:

Masculine		
noun	pronoun	adjective
el hombre	*él*	*guapo*
the man	he	handsome
Feminine		
noun	pronoun	adjective
la mujer	*ella*	*hermosa*
the woman	she	beautiful

See also **gender** in this section.

Gender

Gender means masculine or feminine.

Examples:

Masculine: *el muchacho* / the boy; *el libro* / the book

Feminine: *la muchacha* / the girl; *la casa* / the house

Gerund

In English grammar, a gerund is a word formed from a verb. It ends in *-ing.* Actually, it is the present participle of a verb. However, it is not used as a verb. It is used as a noun. In

Spanish grammar, the infinitive form of the verb is used, as in the example below, when the verb is used as a noun.

Example:
Ver es creer / Seeing is believing [to see is to believe].
  It is sometimes stated as *Ver y creer* [to see and to believe].

The Spanish gerund is also a word formed from a verb. It is the present participle of a verb. The Spanish gerund *[el gerundio]* regularly ends in *-ando* for *-ar* type verbs (of the 1st conjugation), in *-iendo* for *-er* type verbs (of the 2nd conjugation), and *-iendo* for *-ir* type verbs (of the 3rd conjugation). There are also irregular present participles that end in *-yendo*.

Examples of a Spanish gerund:
hablando / talking

comiendo / eating

viviendo / living

If (si) Clause

Another term for an "if" clause is contrary to fact, as in English, if I were king..., if I were rich...

Example:
Si yo tuviera bastante dinero, iría en España. / If I had enough money, I would go to Spain.

Review the imperfect subjunctive of *tener (tuviera)* in §7.7-7 and the conditional of *ir (iría)* in §7.7-8. See also **clause** in this section.

Imperative

The imperative is a mood, not a tense. It is used to express a command. In Spanish it is used in the 2nd person of the singular *(tú)*, the 3rd person of the singular *(usted)*, the 1st person of the plural *(nosotros, nosotras)*, the 2nd person of the plural *(vosotros, vosotras)*, and in the 3rd person of the plural *(ustedes)*.

Review §7.5-17 as well as the forms of the **imperative** (command) in the verb tables in §7.7-8.

Indefinite Article

In English the indefinite articles are *a* and *an*, as in "a book" and "an apple." They are indefinite because they do not refer to any definite or particular noun.

In Spanish there are two indefinite articles in the singular: one in the masculine form *(un)* and one in the feminine form *(una)*.

> **Examples:**
> **Masculine singular:** *un libro* / a book
> **Feminine singular:** *una manzana* / an apple

In the plural they change to *unos* and *unas*.

> **Examples:**
> *unos libros* / some books; *unas manzanas* / some apples

Indefinite Pronoun

An indefinite pronoun is a pronoun that does not refer to any definite or particular noun.

> **Examples:**
> *algo* / something ; *alguien* / someone, somebody

Independent Clause

An independent clause is a group of words that contains a subject and a predicate. It expresses a complete thought when it stands alone.

Example:
El gato está durmiendo sobre la cama. / The cat is sleeping on the bed.

See also **clause**, **dependent clause**, and **predicate** in this section.

Indicative Mood

The indicative mood is used in sentences that make a statement or ask a question. The indicative mood is used most of the time when we speak or write in English or Spanish.

Examples:
¿Adónde vas? / Where are you going?
Voy al cine ahora. / I am going to the movies now.

Indirect Object Noun

An indirect object noun receives the action of the verb *indirectly*.

Example:
Estoy escribiendo un mensaje de texto a Cristina. / I am writing a text message to Christine. *or* I am writing Christine a text message.
The verb is *estoy escribiendo*. The direct object noun is *un mensaje*. The indirect object noun is *Cristina*.

See also **indirect object pronoun** in this section.

Indirect Object Pronoun

An indirect object pronoun takes the place of an indirect object noun. It receives the action of the verb *indirectly*.

Example:
Le escribo una carta a ella. / I am writing a letter to her *or* I am writing her a letter.
The indirect object pronoun is *le* / (to) her. It is clarified by adding *a ella*.

Review the indirect object pronouns, their uses and positions with examples in §6.1-3. See also **indirect object noun** in this section.

Infinitive

An infinitive is a verb form. In English, it is normally stated with the preposition *to*, as in "to talk," "to drink," "to receive." In Spanish, the infinitive form of a verb consists of three major types: those of the 1st conjugation that end in *-ar*, those of the 2nd conjugation that end in *-er*, and those of the 3rd conjugation that end in *-ir*.

In Spanish grammar, the infinitive (*el infinitivo*) is considered a mood.

> **Examples:**
> *hablar* / to talk, to speak
> *beber* / to drink
> *recibir* / to receive

Interjection

An interjection is a word that expresses emotion, a feeling of joy, of sadness, an exclamation of surprise, and other exclamations consisting of one or two words.

> **Examples:**
> *¡Ah!* / Ah! *¡Ay!* / Ouch! *¡Caramba!* / Darn it! *¡Dios mío!* / My God!

Interrogative Adjective

In Spanish, an interrogative adjective is an adjective that is used in a question. As an adjective, it is placed in front of a noun.

> **Examples:**
> *¿Qué libro desea usted?* / What book do you want?
> *¿Qué hora es?* / What time is it?

Interrogative Adverb

In Spanish, an interrogative adverb is an adverb that introduces a question. As an adverb, it modifies the verb.

Examples:
¿Cómo está usted? / How are you?
¿Cuánto cuesta este libro? / How much does this book cost?
¿Cuándo llegará usted? / When will you arrive?

Interrogative Pronoun

An interrogative pronoun is a pronoun that asks a question. There are interrogative pronouns that refer to persons and those that refer to things.

Examples:
¿Quién es? / Who is it?
¿Qué dice usted? / What are you saying?

Interrogative Sentence

An interrogative sentence asks a question.

Example:
¿Qué hace usted? / What are you doing?

Intransitive Verb

An intransitive verb is a verb that does not take a direct object.

Example:
El profesor habla. / The professor is talking.

An intransitive verb takes an indirect object.

> **Example:**
> *El profesor nos habla.* / The professor is talking to us.

See also **direct object pronoun**, **indirect object pronoun**, and **transitive verb** in this section.

Irregular Verb

An irregular verb is a verb that does not follow a fixed pattern in its conjugation in the various verb tenses.

> **Examples of basic irregular verbs in Spanish:**
> *estar* / to be
> *hacer* / to do, to make
> *ir* / to go
> *ser* / to be

See the irregular verb tables in §7.7-8.

Limiting Adjective

A limiting adjective is an adjective that limits a quantity.

> **Example:**
> *tres limones* / three lemons
> *algunos dulces* / a few candies

Main Clause

Main clause is another term for independent clause.

See **independent clause** in this section.

Masculine

In Spanish grammar the gender of a noun, pronoun, or adjective is masculine or feminine, not male or female.

See also **feminine** and **gender** in this section.

Mood of Verbs

Some grammarians use the term *the mode* instead of *the mood* of a verb. Either term means *the manner* or *way* a verb is expressed. In English and Spanish grammar a verb expresses an action or state of being in a particular mood.

In Spanish grammar, there are five moods (*modos*): the infinitive (*el infinitivo*), the indicative (*el indicativo*), the imperative (*el imperativo*), the conditional (*el potencial*), and the subjunctive (*el subjuntivo*).

In English grammar, there are three moods: the indicative mood, the subjunctive mood, and the imperative mood.

Most of the time, in English and Spanish, we speak and write in the indicative mood.

Negative Statement, Affirmative Statement

See **affirmative statement** and **negative statement** in this section.

Neuter

A word that is neuter is neither masculine nor feminine. Common neuter demonstrative pronouns in Spanish are *esto* / this, *eso* / that, *aquello* / that (farther away).

Examples:
¿Qué es esto? / What's this?
¿Qué es eso? / What's that?

For demonstrative pronouns that are not neuter, see **demonstrative pronoun** in this section.

There is also the neuter pronoun *lo*. It usually refers to an idea or statement. It is not normally translated into English but often the translation is "so."

Examples:
¿Estás enferma, María? / Are you sick, Mary?
Sí, lo estoy. / Yes, I am.

No lo creo. / I don't think so.
Lo parece. / It seems so.

Review *lo* in §4.3, §6.4-4, and §12.2.

Noun

A noun is a word that names a person, animal, place, thing, condition or state, or quality.

Examples:
el hombre / the man
la mujer / the woman
el caballo / the horse
la casa / the house
el lápiz / the pencil
la felicidad / happiness
la excelencia / excellence

In Spanish the noun *el nombre* is the word for name and noun. Another word for noun in Spanish is *el sustantivo* / substantive.

Number

In English and Spanish grammar, number means singular or plural.

Examples:

Masc. sing.:	Masc. pl.:
el muchacho / the boy	*los muchachos* / the boys
el lápiz / the pencil	*los lápices* / the pencils
el ojo / the eye	*los ojos* / the eyes

Fem. sing.:	Fem. pl.:
la muchacha / the girl	*las muchachas* / the girls
la casa / the house	*las casas* / the houses
la vaca / the cow	*las vacas* / the cows

Ordinal Number

An ordinal number is a number that expresses position in a series, such as *first, second, third*, and so on. In English and Spanish grammar we talk about 1st person, 2nd person, 3rd person singular or plural regarding subjects and verbs.

See also cardinal number and person (1st, 2nd, 3rd) in this section.

Orthographical Changes in Verb Forms

An orthographical change in a verb form is a change in spelling.

Example:
The verb *conocer* changes spelling in the 1st person singular of the present indicative. The letter *z* is inserted in front of the second *c*. (When formed regularly, the ending *-er* of the infinitive drops and *o* is added for the 1st person singular form of the present indicative. That would result in *conoco*, a peculiar sound to the Spanish ear for a verb form of *conocer*.) The letter *z* is added to keep the sound

of *s* as it is in the infinitive *conocer*. Therefore, the spelling changes
and the form is *yo conozco*. In other forms of *conocer* in the present indicative *z* is not inserted because they retain the sound of *s*.

There are many verb forms in Spanish that contain spelling
changes. See 7.7.

Passive Voice

When we speak or write in the active voice and change to
the passive voice, the direct object becomes the subject, the
subject becomes the object of a preposition, and the verb
becomes *ser* / *to be* plus the past participle of the active verb.
The past participle functions as an adjective.

> **Example:**
> *La ventana fue abierta por el ladrón.* / The window was opened by
> the robber.
> The subject is *la ventana*. The verb is *fue*. The word *abierta* is a
> feminine adjective agreeing with *la ventana*. Actually, it is the past
> participle of *abrir*, but here it serves as an adjective. The object of
> the preposition *por* is *el ladrón*.

See also **active voice** in this section. Compare the above
sentence with the example in the active voice.

Past Anterior Tense

This tense is also called the preterit perfect. See **preterit
perfect tense** in this section and in the Index.

Past Participle

A past participle is derived from a verb. It is used to form the
compound tenses. Its auxiliary verb in English is "to have." In
Spanish, the auxiliary verb is *haber*. It is part of the verb
tense.

Examples:

Infinitive	Present Perfect Indicitive
hablar / to speak, to talk	*he hablado* / I have spoken
comer / to eat	*he comido* / I have eaten
recibir / to receive	*he recibido* / I have received

See also **auxiliary verb** in this section.

Past Perfect Tense

The past perfect tense expresses an action that happened in the past before another past action. This tense is also called the **pluperfect indicative tense**. See §7.5-9.

Person (1st, 2nd, 3rd)

Verb forms in a particular tense are learned systematically according to person (1st, 2nd, 3rd) and number (singular, plural).

Example, showing the present indicative tense of the verb *ir* / to go.

Singular	Plural
1st person: *(yo) voy*	1st person: *(nosotros, nosotras) vamos*
2nd person: *(tú) vas*	2nd person: *(vosotros, vosotras) vais*
3rd person: *(Ud., él, ella) va*	3rd person: *(Uds., ellos, ellas) van*

Personal Pronoun

A personal pronoun is a pronoun that refers to a person. Review the subject pronouns in §6.1-1.

For examples of other types of pronouns, see also **demonstrative pronoun**, **direct object pronoun**, **disjunctive pronoun**, **indefinite pronoun**, **indirect object pronoun**, **interrogative pronoun**, **possessive pronoun**, **reflexive pronoun**, and **relative pronoun** in this section.

Pluperfect Indicative Tense

This tense is also called the past perfect tense. See **past perfect tense** in this section. See also §7.5-9.

Plural

Plural means more than one. See **number** in this section.

Possessive Adjective

A possessive adjective is an adjective that is placed in front of a noun to show possession.

Examples:
mi libro / <u>my</u> book
mis amigos / <u>my</u> friends
nuestra escuela / <u>our</u> school

Possessive Pronoun

A possessive pronoun is a pronoun that shows possession. It takes the place of a possessive adjective with the noun. Its form agrees in gender (masculine or feminine) and number (singular or plural) with what it is replacing.

Examples in English: mine, yours, his, hers, its, ours, theirs

Examples in Spanish:

Possessive Adjective	Possessive Pronoun
mi libro / <u>my</u> book	_el mío_ / mine
mi casa / <u>my</u> house	_la mía_ / mine
mis zapatos / <u>my</u> shoes	_los míos_ / mine

For all the forms of possessive pronouns with examples in Spanish and English, review §6.3.

Predicate

The predicate is that part of the sentence that tells us something about the subject. The main word of the predicate is the verb.

> **Example:**
> *Hoy los turistas van al Museo del Prado.* / Today the tourists are going to the Prado Museum.
>   The subject is *los turistas*. The predicate is *van al Museo del Prado*. The verb is *van*.

Preposition

A preposition is a word that establishes a connection between words.

> **Examples:**
> *con ella* / with her
> *entre tú y yo* / between you and me
> *sin dinero* / without money
> *a México* / to Mexico

Prepositional Pronoun

A prepositional pronoun is a pronoun that is the object of a preposition. The term disjunctive pronoun is also used. For examples, see **disjunctive pronoun** in this section.

Present Participle

A present participle is derived from a verb form. In English, a present participle ends in *-ing*. In Spanish a present participle is called **un gerundio**.

> **Examples:**
> *cantando* / singing
> *comiendo* / eating
> *yendo* / going

For more on present participle usage and formation, see §7.3-2.

Preterit Perfect Tense

This tense is also called the **past anterior**. It is used in formal writing, such as history and literature. See §7.5-10.

Pronoun

A pronoun is a word that takes the place of a noun.

Examples:

el hombre → *él*	*la mujer* → *ella*
the man → he	the woman → she

Reflexive Pronoun and Reflexive Verb

In English a reflexive pronoun is a personal pronoun that contains -*self* or -*selves*. In Spanish and English a reflexive pronoun is used with a verb that is called reflexive because the action of the verb falls on the reflexive pronoun.

Examples:

lavarse / to wash oneself	*(Yo) me lavo.* / I wash myself.
afeitarse / to shave oneself	*Pablo se ha afeitado.* / Paul has shaved himself.

Regular Verb

A regular verb is a verb that is conjugated in the various tenses according to a fixed pattern. See **conjugation** and **irregular verb** in this section.

Relative Pronoun

A relative pronoun is a pronoun that refers to its antecedent.

Example:
La muchacha que está hablando con Juan es mi hermana. / The girl who is talking with John is my sister.
The antecedent is *la muchacha.* The relative pronoun *que* refers to the girl.

See also **antecedent** in this section.

Sentence

A sentence is a group of words that contains a subject and a predicate. The verb is contained in the predicate. A sentence expresses a complete thought.

> **Example:**
> *El tren sale a las dos de la tarde.* / The train leaves at two o'clock in the afternoon.
> The subject is *el tren*. The predicate is *sale a las dos de la tarde*. The verb is *sale*.

See also **complex sentence**, **compound sentence**, and **simple sentence** in this section.

Simple Sentence

A simple sentence is a sentence that contains one subject and one predicate. The verb is the core of the predicate. The verb is the most important word in a sentence because it tells us what the subject is doing.

> **Example:**
> *María está comiendo una manzana de su jardín.* / Mary is eating an apple from her garden.
> The subject is *María*. The predicate is *está comiendo una manzana de su jardín*. The verb is *está comiendo*. The direct object is *una manzana*; *de su jardín* is an adverbial phrase. It tells you from where the apple came.

See also **complex sentence** and **compound sentence** in this section.

Singular

Singular means "one." See **number** in this section.

Spelling Changes in Verb Forms

See **orthographical changes in verb forms** in this section.

Stem of a Verb

The stem of a verb is what is left after we drop the infinitive form ending. The required endings of a regular verb in a particular verb tense are added to the stem.

Infinitive	Ending of Infinitive	Stem
hablar / to talk	*-ar*	*habl*
comer / to eat	*-er*	*com*
escribir / to write	*-ir*	*escrib*

See also **ending of a verb**.

Stem-Changing Verb

In Spanish there are many verb forms that change in the stem.

Example:
The verb *dormir* changes the vowel *o* in the stem to *ue* when the stress (emphasis, accent) falls on that *o*; for example, (*yo*) *duermo*. When the stress does not fall on that *o*, it does not change; for example, (*nosotros*) *dormimos*. Here, the stress is on the vowel *i*.

Subject

A subject is that part of a sentence that is related to its verb. The verb says something about the subject.

Example:
Clara e Isabel son hermosas. / Clara and Isabel are beautiful.
The subject of this sentence is *Clara e Isabel*. To know when to use *e* instead of *y* for *and*, review the entry **conjunction** in this section.

Subjunctive Mood

The subjunctive mood is the mood of a verb that is used in specific cases, e.g., after certain verbs that express a wish, doubt, emotion, fear, joy, uncertainty, an indefinite expression, an indefinite antecedent, certain conjunctions, and others. The subjunctive mood is used more frequently in Spanish than in English.

See also **mood of verbs** in this section.

Subordinate Clause

Subordinate clause is another term for dependent clause. See **dependent clause** in this section.

Superlative Adjective

A superlative adjective is an adjective that expresses the highest degree when making a comparison of more than two persons or things.

Adjective	Comparative	Superlative
bueno / good	*mejor* / better	*el mejor* / the best
alto / tall	*más alto* / taller	*el más alto* / the tallest

See §5.6. See also **comparative adjective** in this section.

Superlative Adverb

A superlative adverb is an adverb that expresses the highest degree when making a comparison of more than two persons or things.

Adverb	Comparative	Superlative
lentamente / slowly	*más lentamente* / more slowly	*lo más lentamente* / the most slowly

See also **comparative adverb** in this section.

Tense of Verb

In English and Spanish grammar, tense means time. The tense of the verb indicates the time of the action or state of being. The three major segments of time are past, present, and future. In Spanish there are fourteen major verb tenses. Seven of them are simple tenses and seven are compound.

For the names of the seven simple tenses and the seven compound tenses in Spanish and English, see the end of §7.5-19.

Transitive Verb

A transitive verb is a verb that takes a direct object.

> **Example:**
> *Cierro la ventana.* / I am closing the window.
>> The subject is *(Yo)*. The verb is *cierro*. The direct object is *la ventana*.

See also **intransitive verb** in this section.

Verb

A verb is a word that expresses an action or a state of being.

> **Examples:**
> **Action:** *Los pájaros están volando.* / The birds are flying.
>> The verb is *están volando*.
>
> **State of being:** *La señora López está contenta.* / Mrs. López is happy. The verb is *está*.

Index

Numbers refer to sections designated by the symbol § in this book. At times, page numbers are given as p. or pp. + number. The abbreviation *ff* means "and the following."

Indispensable for Students . . . Handy for Travelers

Here is a series to help the foreign language student successfully approach verbs and all their details. Complete conjugations of the verbs are arranged one verb to a page in alphabetical order. Verb forms are printed in boldface type in two columns, and common idioms using the applicable verbs are listed at the bottom of the page in each volume. Some titles include a CD-ROM.

501 Verb Series

—————— To order ——————
Available at your local book store
or visit **www.barronseduc.com**

Words to the Wise for Students and Travelers

Here's a great reference book for high school and college students taking Spanish courses and a dependable language aid for travelers to Spanish-speaking countries. This comprehensive bilingual dictionary presents approximately 100,000 words with translations in two separate sections:

- English to Spanish and Spanish to English
- American-style English translations
- Headwords printed in a second color for easy reference with translations, parts of speech, and pronunciation guide printed in black
- Phrases to demonstrate usage follow each definition
- Separate bilingual lists for numerals, phonetic symbols, abbreviations, and geographical names
- Full-color atlas-style maps

- **EXTRA BONUS:**
  Free downloadable bilingual electronic dictionary for your PDA and/or computer

Also featured are concise grammar guides, regular verb conjugation lists, and many more language learning aids.

ISBN-13: 978-0-7641-3329-9
1,328 pages, $16.99, Can$19.99

—And here's a bilingual dictionary designed especially for travelers!

Pocket sized for travelers to fit conveniently in their carry-on flight bags, *Barron's Spanish-English Pocket Dictionary* is also a great reference source for high school and college students taking Spanish. Nearly 70,000 words in two separate sections present:

- American-style English to Spanish and Spanish to English
- Headwords listed with translation, part of speech, and pronunciation
- Phrases to demonstrate usage follow each definition
- Separate bilingual lists present numbers, abbreviations, and more . . .

Abridged from Barron's comprehensive, full-size *Spanish-English Dictionary*, this good-looking pocket reference is an indispensable linguistic tool for travelers and students.

Barron's Educational Series, Inc.
250 Wireless Blvd.
Hauppauge, N.Y. 11788
Call toll-free: 1-800-645-3476

Prices subject to change without notice.

In Canada:
Georgetown Book Warehouse
34 Armstrong Ave.
Georgetown, Ontario L7G 4R9
Call toll-free: 1-800-247-7160

——— To order ———
Available at your
local book store or visit
www.barronseduc.com

(#174) R8